THE BAUHAUS PROJECT I: WEIMAR

Tom Jacobson

BROADWAY PLAY PUBLISHING INC
New York
www.broadwayplaypublishing.com
info@broadwayplaypublishing.com

THE BAUHAUS PROJECT I: WEIMAR
© Copyright 2024 Tom Jacobson

Cover photo by Francisco Hermosillo III

First edition: December 2024
I S B N: 979-8-88856-036-5

Book design: Marie Donovan
Page make-up: Adobe InDesign
Typeface: Palatino

THE BAUHAUS PROJECT I: WEIMAR had its
world premiere on 19 July 2024 at Open Fist Theatre
Company in Los Angeles (produced by Martha
Demson & Amanda Weier with Associate Producer
Nychelle Hawk). The cast and creative contributors
were:

OWEN...Jack Goldwait
ELLIS ....Katarina Joy Lopez
KAI.. John C Sweet
DUCK .... Sang Kim
BREC... Chloe Madriaga

Director .... Martha Demson
Assistant Director... Sarah Zuk
Stage Manager ....John Dimitri
Set design .... Richard Hoover
Lighting design .... Gavan Wyrick
Composer & sound design .... Tim Labor
Costume design...Michael Mullen
Prop design .... Bruce Dickinson, Ina Shumaker
Projection design..Gabrieal Griego

CHARACTERS

ELLIS, *20s-30s, theatre student, Southern accent, also plays:*
    MARIA KIPP, *20s, weaving student*
    ALMA MAHLER GROPIUS, *40s, wife of* WALTER
       GROPIUS, *Viennese accent*
    ADOLF HITLER

BREC, *20s-30s, graphic design student, from Los Angeles,
also plays:*
    GUNTA STÖLZL, *20s, weaving student*

KAI, *20s-30s, fine art student, from New York, also plays:*
    JOHANNES ITTEN, *30s, mystical art teacher, Swiss
       accent, wears glasses*
    ARNOLD SCHÖNBERG, *50s, composer, Viennese accent,
       smokes cigarettes*
    OSKAR SCHLEMMER, *30s, painter, playwright, moves
       like a dancer*

OWEN, *20s-30s, environmental design student, English
accent, also plays:*
    WALTER GROPIUS, *30s, architect*
    PAUL KLEE, *40s, painter, Swiss accent*

DUCK, *20s-30s, ESL music student, strong accent, also
plays:*
    WASSILY KANDINSKY, *50s, painter, Russian accent*
    LYONEL FEININGER, *50s, painter, American accent*
    RICHARD LEUTHEUSSER, *50s, attorney and politician*
    FRITZ ERTL, *20s, a student*

SETTING

The action takes place in an art school in Southern California in the present and in the Bauhaus in Weimar, Germany in the early 1920s.

SPECIAL THANKS

Josh Adams, Cyrus Alexander, Jonathan Bangs, Colin Bates, Bryan Bertone, Lou Danziger, Fran de Leon, Martha Demson, Presciliana Esperolini, Amanda Fekety, Éva Forgács, James Fowler, Ramón Garcia, Nychelle Hawk, Sarah Hollis, Jully Lee, Chelsea Kurtz, West Liang, Ramone Muñoz, Gary Patent, Kacie Rogers, Isabella Roland, David Shofner, Peter James Smith, Michael Sturgis, Donathan Walters, and Dylan Wittrock

ACT ONE

(In a rather plain, ugly space that doesn't matter [dorm room, classroom, meeting room, restaurant, patio, whatever], OWEN, 20s-30s, English accent, wearing a fitted button-down shirt and slacks, reads aloud from a tablet or clipboard:)

OWEN: *(Index finger to temple)* Historically, art schools could not produce unity because art cannot be taught. The fine arts must be merged once more with the workshop, with crafts. When young people who take joy in artistic creation begin their life's work by learning a trade, then the unproductive "artist" will no longer be condemned to dilettantism, for his skill will be preserved in the crafts, attaining excellence and serving man.

(Lights up gradually on BREC, KAI, DUCK and ELLIS all in their 20s or 30s and focused on papers, devices and something they're eating. ELLIS wears boots, a jacket and bright colors. KAI wears black clothes, art shoes and big glasses. DUCK is dressed conservatively but with a touch of color, headphones or earbuds. BREC wears square glasses.)

OWEN: Let us then create a new guild of craftsmen without the class distinctions between craftsman and artist! Together let us desire, conceive and construct a new future, embracing architecture and sculpture and painting—all the arts—in one unity rising toward heaven from the hands of a million workers like the crystal cathedral of a new faith!

(OWEN *stops reading and looks for a reaction. No one is paying attention.*)

OWEN: Inspirational, don't you think?

KAI: *(New York accent)* Sexist.

BREC: *(Some kind of California accent, surfer or Valley or a combo) His* skill! Serving *man!*

KAI: Crafts*man.*

(BREC *takes a photo of* OWEN.)

OWEN: It was 1919!

ELLIS: *(Southern accent, re: food)* Y'all, where did this come from?

OWEN: And translated from German!

BREC: I dunno. My grandmother made it.

(BREC *takes a photo of* ELLIS.)

DUCK: *(International accent)* Most good! Tasty!

(BREC *takes a photo of* DUCK, *who looks at the floor to avoid the photo [and frequently looks floorward thereafter].*)

OWEN: The whole planet was recovering from the First World War and the Spanish Flu—

KAI: *(Crosses arms, a frequent and iconic pose for* KAI*)* Fucking waste of time. I need to be in the studio.

(BREC *takes a photo of* KAI.)

BREC: Painting or sculpture?

ELLIS: I'm so not doing this.

(KAI *shows* BREC *an image on phone, which makes* BREC *wince.*)

BREC: Whoa!

OWEN: It's an assignment. We have to.

KAI: It's rhyparography. Trash art. Bringing the discarded to light in a transparent way.

ELLIS: I'm missing a Shakespeare workshop for this! *(Re: food)* Some kind of meat?

(ELLIS and BREC play around with phones.)

BREC: What's the Bauhaus got to do with, like, communication design?

DUCK: Or music?

ELLIS: What flavor is this, dirt?

OWEN: The Bauhaus had graphic design! A band!

KAI: It was mostly industrial design and architecture.

OWEN: And painting—in the core course.

ELLIS: *(Consulting phone)* Y'all know what a bacculum is?

BREC: *(Hands on hips)* Architecture's your major. Has everyone met Owen? Very famous.

OWEN: Environmental design!

BREC: You do the presentation. You love researching the shit out of everything.

ELLIS: A penis bone.

DUCK: *(Distressed)* Research? Ahhhh!

ELLIS: Walruses have the biggest.

OWEN: Look, for whatever reason we were all assigned this class—

ELLIS: Yeah, what's that about?

BREC: I sure didn't pick it.

DUCK: Is punishment?

KAI: All right, here we go.

BREC: I was up till four working on a packaging assignment—

ELLIS: History is boring! What's a hundred year-old German art school got to do with anything?

OWEN: We're *in* art school.

ELLIS: I never even heard of the Bauhaus before this.

(OWEN *grabs* ELLIS's *mug.*)

ELLIS: Hey!

OWEN: *(Indicates mug)* Bauhaus! *(Grabs something from* BREC*)* Bauhaus!

BREC: Dude!

OWEN: *(Indicates a piece of furniture)* Bauhaus! *(Indicates an appliance)* Bauhaus! *(Indicates architecture of the room)* Bauhaus! *(Grabs* DUCK'S *phone)* Bauhaus! Our own school was founded on Bauhaus principles.

KAI: Okay, okay, we get it.

OWEN: How many of you live in the dorm?

(DUCK *and* ELLIS *raise hands.*)

OWEN: The modern dormitory was invented by the Bauhaus!

BREC: Dorms the Nazis turned into concentration camps.

OWEN: The Bauhaus was *shut down* by the Nazis.

ELLIS: I want to play a Nazi.

DUCK: What is Nazi?

ELLIS: They did the Holocaust.

DUCK: Holocaust?

BREC: *(Astonished)* What?

DUCK: What?

BREC: *(Outraged)* What?!

ELLIS: *(To* DUCK*)* I'll tell you about Nazis later.

BREC: Unbelievable.

ELLIS: It'll make sense when you see me in costume.

OWEN: It's not a play, just a presentation.

ELLIS: Why couldn't it be a play? He didn't specify.

BREC: I thought you weren't doing it.

ELLIS: We shall see.

DUCK: Excuse, please—

OWEN: We can do it as a play if you want. The Bauhaus had a theatre department.

ELLIS: They did?

DUCK: I cannot do play!

OWEN: And music!

DUCK: Oh!

KAI: With all due respect, let's just get this over with. I gotta get my portfolio together for grad school applications.

DUCK: Grad school?	KAI: We know Walter Gropius founded the Bauhaus in 1919—

KAI: —And recruited a bunch of famous artists to teach: Paul Klee, Laszlo Moholy-Nagy—

BREC: *(To* OWEN*)* You're not the only one who knows anything—	KAI: Lyonel Feininger, Marcel Breuer, Wassily Kandinsky—

OWEN: Who played piano and cello—

DUCK: Oh!

OWEN: Yes!	KAI: Oskar Schlemmer—

OWEN: Ran the theatre program—

KAI: Gropius was married to Alma Mahler—

DUCK: Gustav Mahler wife?

OWEN: After.

ELLIS: I want to play Alma Mahler.

BREC: You can't play Alma Mahler *and* a Nazi.

KAI: It's not a play. Just a fucking PowerPoint we can put together in thirty minutes and be done—

ELLIS: I'm not doing it unless it's a play.

KAI: Jesus.

BREC: You want to play Jesus, too?

DUCK: I no play anybody. I play oboe.

BREC: You can compose a Bauhaus song.

OWEN: There actually was one.

DUCK: Like film score? Nino Rota—

ELLIS: Can it be a musical?

DUCK: Bernard Hermann—

OWEN: No, just a play.

DUCK: (*Psycho theme and stabbing*) Ree, ree, ree, ree!

KAI: Fuck it is.

OWEN: Look, I'm happy to write it.

BREC: Don't say "look." It's so aggressive.

OWEN: You needn't do anything except read the lines.

BREC: You always say "look".

ELLIS: I'm memorizing Alma.

OWEN: You always exaggerate.

KAI: With all due respect, I'm not doing a play about a bunch of white people. The Bauhaus is relevant because it influenced modern design—duh—I'm aware of the International Style—

BREC: Transparent glass boxes—

KAI: —But you realize every single one of them was German—

OWEN: Kandinsky was Russian, Klee was Swiss—

KAI: Swiss! You can't get any whiter than that—so not relevant in a contemporary way—

OWEN: Seriously, everyone, you needn't lift a finger. I like research—Gropius, Itten, Klee are kind of my heroes—and it won't take long to write—

ELLIS: I'll direct.

KAI: And play Alma Mahler?

BREC: And a Nazi?

OWEN: Brilliant! It can be as theatrical as you wish.

BREC: You can design a fancy architectural set in the Bauhaus style.

OWEN: You can design the program. And you paint a Kandinsky or a Klee.

KAI: You mean forge?

OWEN: It should be a *gesamtkunstwerk*!

ELLIS: Who can't work?   BREC: You just like saying
                             that.

OWEN: A total work of art, all disciplines together: design, music, dance, painting, sculpture, architecture, theatre—Wagner opera is the classic example—

ELLIS: Or a musical.

DUCK: Excuse, please. Will be…political?

BREC: It has Nazis.

DUCK: Could we…get punish?

ELLIS: If it sucks. Which is why we need a director.

BREC: The assignment is punishment.

ELLIS: Apologies for my breath. I think I've been eating carrion.

DUCK: No, no, I mean—sorry—punish for politic. Public statement— *(Waves phone)* —Video, YouTube…? In my country…

(Silence for a moment)

ELLIS: Ah.

OWEN: We'll be careful.

ELLIS: You mean self-censor?

BREC: You can be a sympathetic Nazi. Fair and balanced.

KAI: We're in college. We can't get punished for our politics—

BREC: Yeah, this is Amurrica!

KAI: You're all registered to vote?

KAI: *(To DUCK)* I know you can't—

BREC: Tomorrow—

OWEN: What good's voting do?

ELLIS: Politics is so awful right now—

KAI: Jesus.

DUCK: But maybe not always in college, in America. I flunk last term. Maybe send home.

KAI: Where YouTube follows. Got it.

DUCK: So cannot flunk again.

OWEN: No, of course not, we can't fail. Even if this isn't a core course for any of us, I'm sure there are real reasons we were assigned—

ELLIS: Punished?

BREC: Do you know something we don't?

OWEN: *(To DUCK)* —So we're not going to let you flunk this term—what's your name?—

DUCK: Duck.

OWEN: Right, Duck. I'm Owen.

BREC: Is that your real name?

BREC: Very famous.

OWEN: None of us are going to flunk. I'll write up some—scenes, I guess—is that right, Herr Direktor—?

ELLIS: Uh…yeah, scenes. That's what they're called—

OWEN: And we can get together later this week to—rehearse, mein Fuhrer?

ELLIS: We can workshop them!

BREC: Heil, you!

(*Lighting change isolates* BREC *and* KAI *in light, the others in darkness.*)

BREC: I have to do this, you know, uncomfortable as it is.

KAI: Uncomfortable?

BREC: My grandmother's a Holocaust survivor.

KAI: Drop the class.

BREC: I can't.

KAI: Why not?

BREC: Academic probation.

KAI: What'd you do?

BREC: (*Beginning a rant*) We were supposed to design a new logo for Fry's Electronics, the ugliest cataclysm of forms I've ever seen in my life. Looks like it was designed by a drunk Klingon. (*Shows logo*) Look at the tragedy of that "s". The apostrophe turns it into an orphan of a bastard font. You could fit Russia between the "r" and the "y". It's the logo equivalent of Tourette's syndrome. I redesigned Planned Parenthood's logo instead.

KAI: Does it need it?

BREC: (*Shows logo*) Looks like it's for a plant food company. So I did this. (*Shows logo*)

KAI: Nice!

BREC: I sent it to Planned Parenthood, and they might even try it out on some materials as a test.

KAI: Design in service of humanity—

BREC: Exactly! But turns out it was a sponsored project. Fry's was expecting free design from everyone in the class, so I got an F. I offered to do extra credit redesigning the Denny's logo in the style of a Polish movie poster of the 1950s, but that just got me deeper in shit. I'm, like, uncooperative. And my mom borrowed money from everybody in her family for my tuition. She'd die if I left school.

KAI: (*Imitating* DUCK) Cannot flunk again.

BREC: Excuse please to take my TOEFL exam. I pay!

KAI: Duck isn't necessarily—

BREC: (*Indicates phone*) Filthy rich parents, conspicuous consumption Instagrams—staring at the camera like a gibbon on Valium—

KAI: What's Owen's deal?

BREC: Like *really* into the Bauhaus.

KAI: You go back a ways?

BREC: Kinda. Are *you* in trouble?

(KAI *shrugs.*)

BREC: I'm trying to scope out this punishment thing.

(KAI *shrugs.* BREC *just stares.*)

KAI: You hear something?

BREC: Rumor of a racist sexist homophobic patriarchal paradigm.

KAI: You forgot fascist.

BREC: So you left a dead raccoon on the prof's desk?

KAI: Roadkill as Recycling! Rhyparography! I followed the assignment guidelines to the letter—it was about transparency to the real—but apparently—like you—I'm uncollaborative.

BREC: Uncooperative.

KAI: So now…Bauhaus.

BREC: You're on punishment, too.

KAI: I guess. Is Owen?

BREC: What do you care about Owen?

KAI: You tell me.

(*They stare at each other a moment.*)

BREC: Dead raccoons are, like, hot.

(*Lights out on them and up on* DUCK.)

DUCK: Why professor assign Bauhaus? I think I find out. Google his address and how you say in English?—*voila*! Was text-tile factory built 1951 by German lady…suspicious. Text-tile design like Bauhaus, but not Bauhaus. Now artist loft for most beloved but mysterious professor. Why he so obsess Bauhaus? German lady Maria Kipp practice Mazdaznan like at Bauhaus!

(*Lights up on everyone. Once again,* BREC *is sharing some kind of food.*)

ELLIS: What's Mazdaznan?

KAI: A cult.

(*Everyone researches on their phones, but* OWEN *of course already knows.*)

OWEN: Johannes Itten, one of the Bauhaus teachers, was the best-known practitioner of Mazdaznan—

KAI: Mazda is the god of light bulbs—

ELLIS: Which was based on Zoroastrianism—

BREC: But who's Maria Kipp?

KAI: Maria Kipp Hand-Loomed Fabrics, 3425 W First Street, Los Angeles—

DUCK: Born 1900, die 1988.

BREC: Drapery and upholstery samples in LACMA's collection—

KAI: Closed 1996.

OWEN: She studied at the *Kunstgewerbeschule* in Munich, not at the Bauhaus—

KAI: The cunt what?

OWEN: *Kunst* is "art" in German. *Kunstgewerbeschule* means—

BREC: You just like saying that, don't you?

OWEN: "Arts and crafts school."

DUCK: Oh—like our school!

KAI: Don't let the teachers hear you say crafts!

BREC: Exactly! They'd shit.

OWEN: Maria Kipp had nothing to do with the Bauhaus.

DUCK: Just our beloved professor house.

ELLIS: Are you suggesting we add this random German lady to our presentation just to suck up to our professor?

DUCK: (*Distressed*) Suck professor?

ELLIS: I'm not above it.

BREC: I bet not.

KAI: All right, here we go.

ELLIS: But—wait—it's kinda genius—maybe there is a link, and if we can connect the dots for our beloved professor—

BREC: Stop calling him that!

DUCK: We no suck at all.

BREC: Are you going to oink out this presentation in your pidgin English? Excuse please, but it is.

DUCK: I read and rememorize. Less suck.

OWEN: Maybe we should do some scenes and find out who sucks.

KAI: The only connection I have with this archaic and esoteric topic is the politics. We could use it to comment on the current situation.

DUCK: No!	KAI: The Nazis closed the Bauhaus, yes?

OWEN: Eventually, after the Bauhaus moved to Berlin, but our assignment is only 1919 to 1923 when the Bauhaus was in Weimar.

ELLIS: Wait, no Nazis?

OWEN: No one paid attention to the Nazis until 1923. They were fighting with the Communists—

ELLIS: I want to play a Communist.	OWEN: But the government of Thuringia became increasingly conservative—

BREC: *(Mocking* OWEN*)* Thuringia!

DUCK: Art! No politic!

KAI: You can't avoid politics. Everything is political.

OWEN: We need to concentrate on school right now—

KAI: Look.

ELLIS: God.

KAI: I know it's hard—right now—to think voting can make a difference, one person can matter, but—

ELLIS: I hate politics!

KAI: Are any of you religious?

ELLIS: Religious?

DUCK: Okay to ask?

ELLIS: What's religion got to do with politics?

KAI: I'm Lutheran. Weird, I know, especially if you've seen my sculpture, but I actually go to church almost every week.

ELLIS: So?

BREC: Really?

KAI: Several years ago I made a small gift to a campaign to persuade the Evangelical Lutheran Church in America to perform same-sex marriages. But I told them don't stop with me. We asked three other people at my little church, and they made gifts. One of them said don't stop with me, let's ask the church council to make a gift. And they did. That summer the national Lutheran assembly voted to accept same-sex marriage. A few years later, when the Supreme Court of the United States of America ruled on same-sex marriage, they cited that the Lutheran Church, the Episcopal Church and the United Church of Christ all accepted same-sex marriage. So my little gift changed the law of the land.

ELLIS: Well, rah-tah-tah-tah-tee.

BREC: That *is* amazing.

ELLIS: If a bit of a stretch. OWEN: Okay, I'll register!

DUCK: Excuse, please—

BREC: I had no idea you were, like, religious. DUCK: But is art school, not politic school!

KAI: School itself is political! Education is political!

DUCK: Back home…my cousin speak politic then speak no more!

ELLIS: What?

KAI: Arrested?

DUCK: Disappear! *(Silence)* No politic!

(Silence)

ELLIS: No politics, y'all.

OWEN: *(After a moment)* Fortunately, the scene I wrote for today has almost no politics. It involves Alma Mahler Gropius—

(Everyone looks to ELLIS, *who grandly takes the pages from* OWEN.*)*

OWEN: And her husband Walter Gropius, founder of the Bauhaus. *(Brandishes pages)* Who wishes to read Walter Gropius? *Architect* Walter Gropius?

BREC: You mean the lead?   KAI: Jesus, just take it.

ELLIS: *(Looking at the pages)* What's a Viennese accent?

OWEN: Like German, I guess.

BREC: We're doing accents? We can't do accents! *(Glance at* DUCK*)* Most of us.

OWEN: *(Overlapping* BREC*)* Alma's from Austria, not Germany like most of the Bauhaus professors, and since we'll all be playing multiple roles I thought the accent would help distinguish her.

KAI: Just pretend you're Sigmund Freud.

BREC: As a woman.

OWEN: Shall we begin?

ELLIS: Use an American accent for Gropius. Or if you must go German, keep it subtle.

(ELLIS *stands to read;* OWEN, *irritated, somewhat reluctantly follows suit.* ELLIS *gives* OWEN *a "Walter" hat and dons an "Alma" wig and picks up a vintage purse.*)

OWEN AS GROPIUS: (*American or subtle German accent*) My dear Alma. Welcome to Weimar.

ELLIS AS MAHLER: (*Viennese accent*) Gropius, you unbelievably silly ass!

(ELLIS AS MAHLER *kisses a surprised* OWEN AS GROPIUS *at length, which is uncomfortable for all.*)

OWEN: I didn't write a kiss!

ELLIS: The director has complete control of the stage directions— (*Goes in for another kiss*)

OWEN AS GROPIUS: (*Quickly, to prevent the kiss*) Welcome to the Bauhaus.

ELLIS AS MAHLER: You flirtatious imp. Have you any Benedictine?

OWEN AS GROPIUS: No.

ELLIS AS MAHLER: Anything to drink at all? I'm utterly parched after my journey.

OWEN AS GROPIUS: No.

ELLIS AS MAHLER: And indescribably shattered by the condition of our son.

OWEN AS GROPIUS: I thought the shunt worked.

ELLIS AS MAHLER: Temporarily. His skull swelled up again, even more hideously than before, monstrous proportions. They can keep draining, but the doctors think he'll live only a few weeks longer.

OWEN AS GROPIUS: He's dying *right now*?

ELLIS AS MAHLER: Not immediately, but…of course it's tremendously expensive…

OWEN AS GROPIUS: Then why are you here in Weimar instead of in Vienna with our—infant child?

ELLIS AS MAHLER: My famous architect husband just opened the Bauhaus…in Weimar. How are all those wonderful artists I introduced you to?

OWEN AS GROPIUS: Kandinsky and Klee are most grateful for the opportunity of a steady income as Masters—

ELLIS AS MAHLER: And your school is instantly prominent because your leading faculty are the two most famous artists in Europe.

OWEN AS GROPIUS: Indeed, we are getting a lot of attention.

ELLIS AS MAHLER: I told you that would work, doubting Thomas. And Johannes Itten?

OWEN AS GROPIUS: He's an odd fellow, but an extremely effective teacher. His introductory class is already oversubscribed.

ELLIS AS MAHLER: I hope you give me credit for him, too. I could have gotten you Klimt if he hadn't died of the Spanish flu.

OWEN AS GROPIUS: Along with fifty million others.

ELLIS AS MAHLER: Did I ever tell you Klimt kissed me?

OWEN AS GROPIUS: Along with fifty million others.

ELLIS AS MAHLER: Have you determined an artistic style for the school? Expressionism is dead, I hear.

OWEN AS GROPIUS: *(Finger to temple)* The Bauhaus isn't a particular style or teaching method, more about connecting art and society with integrity—honestly exposing and celebrating structure, not hiding it behind gewgaws and furbelows—

ELLIS: *(Switches back to* ELLIS, *putting down purse and removing wig)* This is a lot of exposition all at once.

DUCK: What is gewgaw?

BREC: Yeah, furbelow?   OWEN: The presentation needs to be informative. It's educational, not artistic in and of itself.

ELLIS: No one will listen if it's not entertaining.

BREC: Exactly! Like character development, high stakes, conflict!

OWEN: The Bauhaus was super messy, incredibly conflicted, but it led to better art and design.

ELLIS: *(Putting on wig)* Fine art vs. art education. That's the conflict!

KAI: *(Sarcastic) That's* life and death…!

ELLIS: *(Feeling nipples)* Is anyone else cold?

OWEN: May we proceed?

ELLIS AS MAHLER: *(Picking up purse)* Don't you at least have beer?

OWEN AS GROPIUS: No.

ELLIS AS MAHLER: I hear you're already in trouble.

(OWEN AS GROPIUS *picks up a roll of architectural plans, sometimes gesturing with it.)*

OWEN AS GROPIUS: Weimar is the cultural capital of Germany—Goethehaus, Schillerhaus, Liszthaus—but the local Thuringian government is significantly more rigid and old-fashioned than they led me to believe.

ELLIS AS MAHLER: Some scandal, nude swimming in the river?

OWEN AS GROPIUS: The students are young—

ELLIS AS MAHLER: And always throwing their clothes off. How nice for you.

OWEN AS GROPIUS: Alma.

ELLIS AS MAHLER: I'm not the jealous type and neither are you.

OWEN AS GROPIUS: You're not here to congratulate me on the Bauhaus nor to plead for Martin's care—I send plenty of money—

ELLIS AS MAHLER: Tediously direct as always, darling. I'm here to tell you about Werfel.

OWEN AS GROPIUS: How is Franz?

ELLIS AS MAHLER: A fat bowlegged Jew with thick lips and floating slit eyes.

(*Watching,* BREC *reacts.* KAI *notices.*)

OWEN AS GROPIUS: And yet?

ELLIS AS MAHLER: The more he reveals of himself, the more he wins my heart. God, his words!

OWEN AS GROPIUS: (*Fingers to both temples*) Are you here to ask for a divorce?

ELLIS AS MAHLER: (*Laughs charmingly*) Darling, you know I'm too practical for that! But I do have a proposition.

OWEN AS GROPIUS: What?

ELLIS AS MAHLER: I'm still quite fond of you. Proud, even. Manon and I propose—

OWEN AS GROPIUS: Don't drag our daughter into your debaucheries! ELLIS AS MAHLER: —To spend six months of the year here in Weimar and the other six with Franz in Vienna.

OWEN AS GROPIUS: How twentieth-century.

ELLIS AS MAHLER: I actually don't think I could manage more than six months of Franz at a time. He's perverse and insatiable. Before he met me he was destroying himself with maniacal self-abuse, three times a day since he was ten. He's always exhausted, his cells degenerated, softening the brain. I've prohibited him from solo gratification for his own good. But he continues to report relapses.

OWEN AS GROPIUS: You know I'm neither a prude nor a saint. But this time-share proposal would publicly humiliate all three of us.

ELLIS AS MAHLER: Werfel's begging me to return, can think of nothing but Martin's condition, the child's inevitable fate—

OWEN AS GROPIUS: I still admire Werfel. Such tenderness for his rival's son.

ELLIS AS MAHLER: His own son.

OWEN AS GROPIUS: Ah.

ELLIS AS MAHLER: Surely you've done the math, Herr Architect. Martin's weakness comes from Werfel's degenerate seed, my pathetic little Jew-baby.

(BREC *reacts.*)

OWEN AS GROPIUS: I've pretended he was mine for your sake and the child's.

ELLIS AS MAHLER: What do I care about the elegant gentleman with brightly colored spats who just happens to be married to me? I am not a Gropius, I cannot call myself Gropius. I'm Mahler for all eternity. Are you sure there's no Benedictine?

OWEN AS GROPIUS: If you're trying to abuse me into asking you for a divorce, you'll have to give me custody of Manon.

ELLIS AS MAHLER: You might as well put a revolver to my head!

OWEN AS GROPIUS: Don't tempt me! You're nothing to me now but a superannuated bit of pelvis!

ELLIS AS MAHLER: Werfel finds me fresh enough. But the perversions he subjects me to! Gets me so aroused I can't sleep. Last night on the train I kept imagining him with cripples, intoxicated myself with them, a one-legged woman, me as a spectator but so boundlessly excited I had to lay a hand on myself—

OWEN AS GROPIUS: Alma, enough—

ELLIS AS MAHLER: The more significant the man, the sicker his sexuality.

OWEN AS GROPIUS: You must return to Vienna immediately. Your son is dying, his father needs you to hump a stump—

ELLIS AS MAHLER: Darling, I've only just arrived in Weimar! And tonight's the party for Schönberg!

OWEN AS GROPIUS: You starfucker! Another famous Jew for your collection. His wife is here. Not that that's ever stopped you!

BREC: Whoa, whoa, whoa!

KAI: Yeah, the anti-Semitism!

(ELLIS *removes the wig and puts down the purse.*)

OWEN: They were all anti-Semites in those days!

DUCK: What is starfucker?

BREC: Anachronistic!

KAI: With all due respect, so is "time share."

OWEN: I took some liberties with the translation.

ELLIS: It's kinda supercalifragilistic! They had skinny-dipping just like we do! Does Alma stay for the party? Maybe she gets naked!

BREC: You can't be Alma Mahler, a Nazi *and* naked.

ELLIS: You know, to show her vulnerability, a metaphor—

KAI: Or a pathetic attempt to be shocking.

ELLIS: Alma liked shocking people!

OWEN: This can't be all about Alma Mahler. She was only around at the beginning of the Bauhaus. But you see the problem: there's so much we'll have to leave out.

ELLIS: I'm the director: I get to choose!

BREC: It's everybody's grade.

OWEN: The writer decides!

KAI: All right, here we go.

(OWEN *produces more pages.*)

OWEN: Gunta Stolzl was the only female Master at the Bauhaus, and she started as a student. Most of this is pretty speculative—based on Duck's research about Maria Kipp—

(ELLIS *grabs some pages.*)

BREC: You can't be everybody!

DUCK: (*Cheerfully*) Starfucker!

ELLIS: We shall see.

OWEN: (*To* BREC) I was thinking you could be Gunta.

ELLIS: (*Donning a "Maria" wig*) And I'll be the mysterious Maria Kipp. Any accent?

OWEN: Maybe just tamp down your own.

ELLIS: *(Picks up a mug of tea to become* KIPP*)* I ain't got no accent!

BREC AS STOLZL: *(Donning a "Gunta" head scarf)* Maria, how was your journey from Munich? Is Erich not with you?

(Spontaneous elaborate hugging ritual. ELLIS' KIPP *is much more reserved than* MAHLER*, with upright posture and a dry manner.* BREC AS STOLZL *picks up a sketchbook and a swath of fabric.)*

ELLIS AS KIPP: The journey was pleasant enough. Wonderful to see you, Gunta, after all these months. How is the Bauhaus?

BREC AS STOLZL: *(Precise enunciation)* We're working very hard, but there are an awful lot of parties. There's one tonight to welcome Arnold Schönberg.

ELLIS AS KIPP: Is he a famous artist?

BREC AS STOLZL: *(Hands extended in enthusiasm)* A composer. Kandinsky is beside himself with excitement. They worked together in the Blue Rider group before the war. Where's Erich?

ELLIS AS KIPP: In Munich.

BREC AS STOLZL: I wanted him to meet Johannes Itten.

ELLIS AS KIPP: Who's that?

BREC AS STOLZL: Our best teacher, Swiss, a mystic. But why isn't Erich—?

ELLIS AS KIPP: I might be leaving him, Gunta. I haven't decided yet.

BREC AS STOLZL: Oh, dear. When will you know?

ELLIS AS KIPP: I expect to learn a lot about myself away from him—for the first time since I was a girl, really. Perhaps I'll stay here at the Bauhaus.

BREC AS STOLZL: I wish you would! We don't have nearly enough girls. Why don't you audit Itten's introductory course?

ELLIS AS KIPP: Am I allowed?

BREC AS STOLZL: If Itten says it's all right. He's quite a character with his robe and shaved head, but strangely handsome!

ELLIS AS KIPP: His robe?

BREC AS STOLZL: He practices Mazdaznan, a new religion based on ancient Persian Zoroastrianism, very strict, vegetarian, with enemas and sexual discipline.

ELLIS AS KIPP: Enemas?

BREC AS STOLZL: And sexual discipline! Some them even cut themselves to let impurities flee the body as pus.

ELLIS AS KIPP: Some of them? How many are there?

BREC AS STOLZL: About twenty students turned Mazdaznan.

ELLIS AS KIPP: Have you?

BREC AS STOLZL: I fear I'm not strong enough for it. Itten has a powerful presence. Once, in his class, I fainted!

ELLIS AS KIPP: Fainted? Do you like it here?

BREC AS STOLZL: I can no longer separate my destiny from the Bauhaus. I've learned so much already about materials, designing an object for its purpose and with respect for human scale—so much intelligent, moral and generous thinking! Everything we do here is a total work of art, all the arts combined to transform society.

ELLIS AS KIPP: That sounds exhausting. I just want to weave.

BREC AS STOLZL: I had to find rooms with looms in town, beg leftover fabric and thread, lace, veils. We're desperately poor and deliriously happy! We have to make our own fabric dyes.

ELLIS AS KIPP: Out of what?

BREC AS STOLZL: Betel nut, woad, indigo, cochineal—

ELLIS AS KIPP: Cochineal, what's that?

BREC AS STOLZL: Ground up insects!

ELLIS AS KIPP: What color results?

BREC AS STOLZL: Their bodies are twenty percent carminic acid, so the dye is brilliant shades of crimson and scarlet!

ELLIS AS KIPP: I find commercial dyes insufficiently vivid.

BREC AS STOLZL: Cochineal can be very bright. Oh, Maria, it's wonderful you're here! I find myself bursting to create, building instead of sitting at a cultural apex when everything is already finished. Isn't it marvelous to make things? To bring something entirely new into the world? Like having a baby—

ELLIS AS KIPP: But with much more control.

BREC AS STOLZL: Yes, Maria, yes! I can't wait for you to take Itten's class!

ELLIS AS KIPP: I look forward to fainting.

OWEN: Perfect!

ELLIS: I hope y'all noticed my Maria's dry and stoic personality contrasts with Alma's more effusive presence.

KAI: Your Alma's wet all the time.

BREC: Like what's with all the cliches: the adoring art acolyte, the insane but charismatic art teacher—

KAI: The Bauhaus *invented* cliches.

BREC: Do we need a narrator? These character scenes are cute but we could make the most important points more efficiently by just saying them.

ELLIS: But not effectively! If they're emotionally engaged, the audience will remember better.

OWEN: Duck, what do you think?

DUCK: Very funny sometime, sometime touch my— *(Indicates heart)* —Touch me.

KAI: That would be Alma, always touching everyone.

OWEN: I like your idea of a narrator, not to shortcut the emotion but to ground us in facts, clarify the politics.

DUCK: No politic!

(BREC starts working on phone.)

OWEN: Gropius can narrate.

KAI: The Bauhaus was besieged from every side. Isn't that the political point?

DUCK: No politic!!

BREC: No politic? What's this then?

(BREC shows phone to DUCK.)

DUCK: Not my post!

ELLIS: Mean!

OWEN: You should play Johannes Itten.

(OWEN hands KAI pages.)

KAI: I am not shaving my head!

OWEN: Just use your best Swiss accent. And these.

(OWEN hands KAI wire rim glasses. After a moment, KAI puts them on. OWEN picks up the rolled plans to become GROPIUS.)

OWEN AS GROPIUS: My dear Johannes, there's been another complaint.

KAI AS ITTEN: *(Swiss accent, very soft, not bad)* Fainting.

OWEN AS GROPIUS: You noticed.

KAI AS ITTEN: She fell onto the begonia she was drawing. Crushed it.

OWEN AS GROPIUS: *(Finger to temple)* It's that garlic mush you've got us all eating. The students are undernourished, their skin turning gray! Not everyone at the Bauhaus is Mazdaznan.

KAI AS ITTEN: Bauhaus is a style of life, not a style of architecture or design. Mazdaznan is healthy and pure.

OWEN AS GROPIUS: Our reputation nowadays is fainting, farting and bad breath. When we should be known for creating affordable design for the people.

KAI AS ITTEN: We're creating artistic genius!

OWEN AS GROPIUS: Both! Absolutely! One leads naturally to the other.

KAI AS ITTEN: *(Smiles oddly)* The Silver Prince.

OWEN AS GROPIUS: What?

KAI AS ITTEN: What Klee calls you. The diplomat.

OWEN AS GROPIUS: As you can imagine, there are so many competing interests when you're running a school: fainting students, underpaid Masters and the Thuringian Landtag registers petty policy violations almost daily—many enemies—

KAI AS ITTEN: Richard Leutheusser.

OWEN: What? No— *(Looks at KAI's script)* —The line is—

KAI: I'm improvising.

BREC: Ooh, real conflict!

DUCK: What?

ELLIS: Awesome!

KAI AS ITTEN: You met with Leutheusser yesterday.

OWEN AS GROPIUS: *(Also improvising, uncomfortably)* Well, yes, he was here.

KAI AS ITTEN: Otherwise one neurasthenic fainter wouldn't capture your attention.

OWEN AS GROPIUS: All students are family—

KAI AS ITTEN: Politicians will be the death of the Bauhaus! Ignore them!

OWEN AS GROPIUS: Or…what?

(KAI AS ITTEN *just smiles his odd smile.*)

ELLIS: Ooh, creepy!

OWEN: Well, that certainly went a bit off the rails.

BREC: That's when it came to life.

OWEN: We can't improvise the entire presentation, just make up facts as they spontaneously—combust!

KAI: Why not?

DUCK: We must pass course.

OWEN: Indeed!

DUCK: Must dot our Ps and Qs.

ELLIS: But maybe we could improvise scenes while we develop the play.

OWEN: That would mean everyone doing at least some of the research.

KAI: I'm cool with that. I researched Leutheusser.

OWEN: May I confer with the director?

DUCK: *(To KAI)* How long grad school?

KAI: Most MFA programs are two or three years, but for a PhD you can drag it out almost a decade.

DUCK: Ten years!

KAI: If you work it right, you can be a student forever.

(Lighting change isolates OWEN *and* ELLIS *in light, everyone else disappears in darkness.)*

ELLIS: *Quel disaster!*

OWEN: It's going okay. Aside from Duck hardly speaking English.

ELLIS: Kai doesn't take direction and every time Brec comes in the room I hear theremin music.

OWEN: Just focused on graphics—

ELLIS: Posted all our photos online without permission—

OWEN: Yeah, that's Brec.

ELLIS: —Except yours.

OWEN: I've a blackmail photo in reserve to retaliate.

ELLIS: And what's with the "very famous" crap?

OWEN: Think of it as a form of intimacy.

ELLIS: Invasive and hostile! To Duck and particularly to you.

OWEN: That's why you're the director.

ELLIS: Not because I suck as an actor?

OWEN: You're the only actor among us!

ELLIS: My acting teacher called me unfocused, taking acting, directing, set design—a "flailing dilettante" in his exact words! Flailing! *(Flails)* Can you believe it? God!

OWEN: You're an undergraduate. You're supposed to be a dilettante. You're supposed to flail.

ELLIS: No one in class wants to do scenes with me. One of them said I acted like a Southern game show host. If no teacher takes me next term for acting, I'm out. Just like at UCLA, USC, Occidental and LACC!

OWEN: LACC?

ELLIS: My dad says this is my last chance.

OWEN: Lots of actors have big careers without talent.

ELLIS: I have talent. This Bauhaus thing will give me a chance to prove it.

OWEN: Prove it to who? Your father?

ELLIS: Our advisors! They're all coming to the presentation. You didn't know?

OWEN: (*Didn't know*) They just don't understand you. As Walter Gropius said, "One must always remain in opposition in order to stay fresh."

ELLIS: We need a Nazi.

OWEN: That would be Brec. If Brec weren't Jewish.

ELLIS: Aha! It *is* personal.

OWEN: We have some history.

ELLIS: (*Pause*) History? No details, no nuance?

OWEN: You direct on stage, I'll direct off.

ELLIS: We shall see.

(*Lighting change. Everyone has pages.* BREC *has food.* KAI *has donned a suitcoat and grabbed a cigarette to become a new character,* ARNOLD SCHÖNBERG, *whose eyes tend to bug out.* ELLIS AS MAHLER *makes sure everyone has a glass of champagne.* DUCK *dons a cardigan and adopts a ramrod posture [no longer looking shyly at the floor] to become* KANDINSKY.)

KAI AS SCHÖNBERG: (*Viennese accent, baritone, smoking cigarette*) A work of art is a living organism, complete in itself. Every detail reveals its essence, the whole can be known from the part. Just as when you cut into the human body—what comes out?

(Only slightly ostentatiously, DUCK drops the pages, having memorized the whole scene.)

DUCK AS KANDINSKY: *(Russian accent)* Blood!!

KAI AS SCHÖNBERG: From a drop of blood, a single hair, a scraping of skin, you can know the whole body, the whole personality. By the same token, one phrase of music can encapsulate a symphony—

(KAI AS SCHÖNBERG sings a few very familiar notes, possibly Beethoven's Fifth Symphony, to illustrate the point. ELLIS transforms briefly from MAHLER to KIPP, switching wigs and picking up the mug of tea.)

ELLIS AS KIPP: This is Arnold Schönberg?

BREC AS STOLZL: Yes, shhh!

KAI AS SCHÖNBERG: One splash of pigment an entire painting—

OWEN AS GROPIUS: *(Finger to temple)* One window a palace—

BREC AS STOLZL: One thread a tapestry—

(ELLIS transforms back to MAHLER, a little drunk.)

ELLIS AS MAHLER: One scrotum a nude!

(Everyone looks at her.)

ELLIS AS MAHLER: A sculpture, a nude sculpture, of course. A marble scrotum, not a real scrotum.

(ELLIS transforms instantly into KIPP.)

ELLIS AS KIPP: And who is that?

OWEN AS GROPIUS: Alma, that's enough body parts.

BREC AS STOLZL: Alma Mahler Gropius, married to the Director! She drinks.

OWEN AS GROPIUS: Herr Schönberg, we are most honored by your presence. Your visit has focused all of Germany on the Bauhaus this week.

(OWEN AS GROPIUS *raises a glass, all do*)

OWEN AS GROPIUS: To Arnold Schönberg, Germany's greatest composer!

(ELLIS *switches back to* MAHLER.)

ELLIS AS MAHLER: Greater than Mahler?

OWEN AS GROPIUS: Greatest *living* composer!

ELLIS AS MAHLER: I am just joking, Gropius. He's Austrian like me! Aren't you, Herr Schönberg?

DUCK AS KANDINSKY: Schönberg is international, such as me!

(ELLIS *becomes* KIPP *and confers with* STOLZL *as everyone else sips champagne.*)

ELLIS AS KIPP: Who's the Russian?

BREC AS STOLZL: The most famous artist in Europe!

ELLIS AS KIPP: Picasso?

BREC AS STOLZL: Wassily Kandinsky!

KAI AS SCHÖNBERG: With great relish I devoured Kandinsky's book, *Concerning the Spiritual in Art*, which paves the road for paintings of the future.

(ELLIS *switches back to* MAHLER, *a bit drunker.*)

ELLIS AS MAHLER: You've quite an admirer, Comrade Kandinsky!

OWEN AS GROPIUS: Alma, rude!

DUCK AS KANDINSKY: I am not the communist, Frau Gropius, which you well know. The Bolsheviks starve my young son to death.

ELLIS AS MAHLER: My young son is dying in Vienna as we speak, and where is his father?

(Wig change: ELLIS *instantly becomes* KIPP.*)*

ELLIS AS KIPP: She's horrid!

BREC AS STOLZL: Isn't she?

DUCK AS KANDINSKY: I condolence you both.

OWEN AS GROPIUS: No condolence needed, in my case.

ELLIS AS KIPP: How awkward!

BREC AS STOLZL: You have no idea.

DUCK AS KANDINSKY: But also I return with joy Herr Schönberg admiration. In 1911 I have great privilege to hear concert of three piano piece of Schönberg that totally destroy tonality and structure. So brilliant I turn into painting!

*(*ELLIS *turns into* MAHLER.*)*

ELLIS AS MAHLER: Comrade, you're making Schönberg blush! *(Touching* SCHÖNBERG*)* You're scarlet! Or is that crimson? *("Russian" accent)* Some shade of red.

OWEN AS GROPIUS: *(Deftly taking* MAHLER's *drink)* Wassily, what was that painting inspired by Schönberg?

DUCK AS KANDINSKY:	ELLIS AS MAHLER:
Impression: Concert. A black block, the piano, floating on a yellow sound—	Gropius, give me my drink!

(They tussle over the drink as KANDINSKY *goes on about art. When* GROPIUS *gets the drink,* ELLIS *turns into* KIPP.*)*

DUCK AS KANDINSKY:	ELLIS AS KIPP:
In this piece, Schönberg break with tonality.	This is Viennese sophistication?

DUCK AS KANDINSKY:	BREC AS STOLZL:
Based on the first three notes, vertical harmony—	She's slept with every artist and composer—

now she's starting on writers.

(ELLIS *turns into* MAHLER.)

ELLIS AS MAHLER: Herr Schönberg, I'm forever grateful for your defense of Mahler's Second Symphony. The critics called my first husband banal, sentimental—

KAI AS SCHÖNBERG: When I heard the Second Symphony, I was gripped with passion, my heart pounded like a beast seeking escape. The mind is tentative, unsure, doesn't trust the sensual, much less the supersensual—

ELLIS AS MAHLER: (*Touching him with her pinky*) Ah, yes, Schonberg, the supersensual! Only a Jew can fully appreciate Mahler—!

DUCK AS KANDINSKY: When I hear music I see colors!

OWEN AS GROPIUS: Synesthesia?

DUCK AS KANDINSKY: (*Struggling with pronunciation*) Yes, synthetic—symphonesia—

OWEN AS GROPIUS: When I hear numbers I see colors. For instance, three is blue, four brown, seven forest green, eleven silver—

ELLIS AS MAHLER: (*Making fun of* GROPIUS) Twelve fuschia, thirteen ecru—

KAI AS SCHÖNBERG: (*Terrified*) Ahhhh!

DUCK AS KANDINSKY: Schönberg, what is wrong?

OWEN AS GROPIUS: BREC AS STOLZL:
Alma, what've you done?   Give him air!

KAI AS SCHÖNBERG: The number! The number! She said the number!

DUCK AS KANDINSKY: In Russia thirteen is unlucky.

KAI AS SCHÖNBERG: Don't say it! It's evil!

ELLIS AS MAHLER: What's wrong with thirteen?

KAI AS SCHÖNBERG: Ahhh!

OWEN AS GROPIUS: BREC AS STOLZL:
Alma, shut up!   No more counting!

ELLIS AS MAHLER: How about multiples? Twenty-six?

KAI AS SCHÖNBERG: Ahhh!

ELLIS AS MAHLER: Thirty-nine?

KAI AS SCHÖNBERG: Stop, I beg you!

BREC AS STOLZL: It's a phobia!

DUCK AS KANDINSKY: Is like synsenesia—
synchromesia—thinesthia—?

(DUCK *gives up and breaks character, tearing off the
cardigan.*)

DUCK: I cannot do!

OWEN: Brilliant! That Russian accent!

DUCK: Excuse, please.

ELLIS: And you had it all memorized, fabuloso!

DUCK: I fail. Fucking English.

ELLIS: That's actually the only English word you need
to know.

ELLIS: Fuck functions   OWEN: Let's move on,
as a noun, a verb, an   one more scene—
adjective, an adverb—

KAI: Another one? Can't we cut anything?

BREC: Exactly! Is Mahler in this one, too?

OWEN: Yes…

ELLIS: Hey!   BREC: A little Alma goes a
                                long way.

ELLIS: *(Grabbing pages)* You can't cut Alma!

DUCK: *(To* KAI*)* Musician never quote— *(Hums same clichéd notes* KAI *did as* SCHÖNBERG*)*

KAI: *(Ignoring* DUCK*, irritated)* What's the scene?

OWEN: *(Handing pages)* Alma and Schönberg tete-a-tete immediately following.

ELLIS AS MAHLER: *(Toasted)* Gropius trained military dogs in the war. I couldn't bear to write letters addressed to Head of the Canine School. Told him I wouldn't touch anything he sent me unless he assured me he washed before he handled it. I was horrified by the thought of him surrounded by filthy animals.

KAI AS SCHÖNBERG: *(Uncomfortable, smoking cigarette)* Is this what you wished to tell me?

ELLIS AS MAHLER: No, you flirtatious imp. *(Smiles seductively)* Be careful of Kandinsky.

KAI AS SCHÖNBERG: He's my oldest friend in Germany!

ELLIS AS MAHLER: But Russian, not German, not Austrian. He only knows Jews of the *shtetl*—

ELLIS AS MAHLER:	KAI AS SCHÖNBERG:
—Not cultured, assimilated Jews of Vienna.	What are you accusing him of?

ELLIS AS MAHLER: I was married to a Jew. I know anti-Semitism when I hear it. Mahler's suffering at the hands of Aryan critics sensitized me to the subtleties.

KAI AS SCHÖNBERG: I've never heard him say one thing—

ELLIS AS MAHLER: Not kike or yid or blood libel, but perhaps he's complained of Orientalizing or bankers or called someone pushy—

KAI AS SCHÖNBERG: Nothing like that!

ELLIS AS MAHLER: He enjoys Wagner.

KAI AS SCHÖNBERG: Many enjoy Wagner, even Jews, I hear.

ELLIS AS MAHLER: You hear?

KAI AS SCHÖNBERG: I became a Lutheran in 1898.

ELLIS AS MAHLER: Mahler became Catholic! But you are always Jewish as well, the eternal Jew.

(ELLIS AS MAHLER *smiles, reaches out with her little finger and touches* KAI AS SCHÖNBERG, *who freezes.*)

ELLIS AS MAHLER: Bite me. Bite me like a man kitty.

(KAI AS SCHÖNBERG *remains frozen, horrified. No one reacts for a moment.*)

BREC: That's like super creepy.

DUCK: Man kitty?   KAI: Yeah, let's cut it.

ELLIS: No! It will make an impression! Foreshadowing!

DUCK: I no understand. Orientalizing?

BREC: It's code. When someone in LA says "Westsider" they mean Jewish.

KAI: We've hardly touched on the important figures: Feininger, Muche, Klee, Schlemmer, Mies van der Rohe, Breuer, Bayer, the Albers—

BREC: Exactly, what about Barcelona chairs? They're important!

DUCK: Important chairs?

BREC: And I'm a little surprised you'd go out of your way to make Kandinsky look anti-Semitic. Isn't he one of your art gods?

OWEN: They're all my heroes, not gods, I think we should be honest—

KAI: Transparent!

OWEN: Yes!

ELLIS: All Germans are racist!

(*Awkward silence*)

DUCK: Um…

BREC: All Germans?

KAI: That's kinda racist.

BREC: Kinda?

DUCK: German is race?

OWEN: Okay, we can cut it.

ELLIS: No!

KAI: With all due respect, Alma has a way of taking over.

BREC: We should cut her altogether.

OWEN: She doesn't have a lot of bearing on the larger story—

ELLIS: She has life! She's passionate and funny and yes a little crazy but we don't want people to fall asleep!

DUCK: We want good grade.

ELLIS: (*To* BREC) You're shitting all over Owen's writing cause you had a bad break-up—

DUCK: What?   KAI: Ah!

OWEN: That's irrelevant—   BREC: None of your
                          business, Ellis!

(BREC *and* ELLIS *aggressively photograph each other.*)

BREC: Or maybe it is! What was Alma's improvised kiss about?

ELLIS: You're jealous!

BREC: I broke up with   OWEN: Jealous? What?
Owen!

ELLIS: But nobody ever talks about cause why? You got something on Owen?

KAI: Shut the fuck up,   DUCK: Excuse please,
everybody, goddammit.   excuse.

ELLIS: Let Duck talk!

DUCK: I have idea.

(Everyone gives DUCK *their attention, albeit impatiently.)*

DUCK: Maybe one more scene with all characters, then decide? Must not split baby with the bathwater.

KAI: *(After a moment)* Do you have one like that?

OWEN: I do. The Bauhaus celebrated everything with a party. All the characters attend, plus everyone we haven't seen yet, Paul Klee, Otto Schlemmer, Lyonel Feininger, etcetera.

BREC: What kind of party?

ELLIS: A costume party!

DUCK: And I write song!

ELLIS: *(Sniffing armpit)* You could score it like a movie!

KAI: *(Consulting phone)* Or give each character a theme song.

DUCK: Leitmotif! Wagner!

BREC: This isn't an opera.

DUCK: *(Pronouncing it with difficulty)* Gesamt…Kunst… Verk!

KAI: How about this for Mahler? *(Plays naughty music on phone)*

OWEN: We may not have time for music.

DUCK: No time for music?   OWEN: Our presentation is
                           due in ten days.

ELLIS: *(Offering armpit to* KAI*)* Does this smell like hamburger to you?

(Lights out on everyone but OWEN *and* BREC.*)*

OWEN: Nothing's going on between me and Ellis!

BREC: Is Ellis aware of that?

OWEN: I've given no—encouragement—!

BREC: Does Ellis know your financial situation?

OWEN: Ellis doesn't know me!

BREC: Or your arrangement?

OWEN: Please don't fuck this up. Sit on the sidelines and carp— You've no idea how hard it is to lead— anything—

BREC: Lead? If naive optimism is leadership—

OWEN: Leaders sacrifice—sometimes their dignity, sometimes more—

BREC: You can't just manipulate—bully us into—

OWEN: *(Produces a green envelope)* I know you don't care one whit about the Bauhaus or my future—

BREC: *(Taking envelope)* What's this?

OWEN: The legendary green envelope. Some schools have a tradition of rush parties—we have—

BREC: Kinda retro creepy.

OWEN: Official warning of pending expulsion.

BREC: *(Reading)* "For delinquent tuition…"

OWEN: You haven't received one?

BREC: I'm not delinquent.

OWEN: In payment.

BREC: I'm not a bitch. You're acting like I'm a bitch.

OWEN: I know your mother. You need the grade almost as badly as I do. You should design the program for our presentation.

(BREC shrugs.)

OWEN: And impressing Kai with graphic design wouldn't hurt.

BREC: Maybe you're the jealous one.

OWEN: This is more important than us. Let's just get through this, please. Then we never have to see each other again.

(*Lighting change reveals* ELLIS AS MAHLER *in costume as a Valkyrie,* DUCK AS KANDINSKY *dressed as an antenna and* KAI AS ITTEN *costumed as an amorphous monster. All costumes appear to be quick improvisations. Throughout the scene they may confer with script pages or abandon them.* ELLIS AS MAHLER *makes sure everyone has drinks, but mostly* MAHLER.)

ELLIS AS MAHLER: Herr Itten, what in the world are you dressed as?

KAI AS ITTEN: A monster.

(BREC *and* OWEN *don costumes.*)

DUCK AS KANDINSKY: Same as you, Frau Gropius.

ELLIS AS MAHLER: Pray do not call me Gropius! Call me Grimgerde!

BREC AS STOLZL: (*Dressed as a tapestry, serving food*) Master Kandinsky, are you an antenna?

DUCK AS KANDINSKY: I think so. You are flag?

BREC AS STOLZL: A tapestry!

OWEN AS GROPIUS: (*Dressed "French"*) Johannes, may I have a word?

(DUCK *changes into a costume of two triangles.*)

KAI AS ITTEN: Who are you?

ELLIS AS MAHLER: He's supposed to be Le Corbusier, but he looks like a mime!

OWEN AS GROPIUS: *(Fingers to temples)* I've another complaint.

KAI AS ITTEN:
No one's fainted!

ELLIS AS MAHLER:
Gunta, you're so fetching in that *schmata*.

OWEN AS GROPIUS:
Not a student, a minor Thuringian official trying to make a name for himself.

BREC AS STOLZL:
It's not a *schmata*!

(OWEN AS GROPIUS pulls KAI AS ITTEN aside and they both change costumes. Dressed as triangles and wearing a broad-brimmed hat, DUCK has become LYONEL FEININGER, who clasps one hand over the other.)

ELLIS AS MAHLER: So geometric, Lyonel! Do you represent American capitalism?

DUCK AS FEININGER: *(Exaggerated American accent)* It's a spiritual conundrum: I can't decide whether to be isosceles, equilateral or acute.

ELLIS AS MAHLER: You're acute to me!

(ELLIS changes costume to become KIPP. KAI becomes OSKAR SCHLEMMER, graceful despite an awkward costume, with a tenor voice and a mask worn on top of his head.)

DUCK AS FEININGER: Herr Schlemmer, are you an Italian fascist?

KAI AS SCHLEMMER: *(Sticks attached to arms)* I'm Monsieur Le Corbusier's best friend— *(Poses perpendicularly)* The right angle. Dull and concrete compared to Master Klee.

DUCK AS FEININGER: What are you, Paul?

(OWEN has become PAUL KLEE, wearing a bow tie and smoking a pipe.)

OWEN AS KLEE: *(Swiss accent, mystical)* The song of the blue tree.

DUCK AS FEININGER: Very spiritual!

ELLIS AS KIPP: *(With a weird hat)* Gunta, is that Paul Klee?

(DUCK changes back to the KANDINSKY costume. OWEN AS KLEE and KAI AS SCHLEMMER pose.)

BREC AS STOLZL: Oh, Maria, that Mahler bitch called me a *schmata*!

ELLIS AS KIPP: You're a Gobelin tapestry! Anyone could see it!

ELLIS AS KIPP/BREC AS STOLZL: Not a *schmata*!

KAI AS SCHLEMMER: I might turn this into a ballet. What do you think?

DUCK AS KANDINSKY: She called me an anti-Semite!

OWEN AS KLEE: Now we are a ballet school?

BREC AS STOLZL: To your face?

(ELLIS changes back to MAHLER. KAI changes back to ITTEN.)

DUCK AS KANDINSKY: I pick up on antenna.

BREC AS STOLZL: Master Klee, is it possible to sing the song of the blue tree?

DUCK AS KANDINSKY: I play on cello!

OWEN AS KLEE: It is the sound of the azure sap sweetly surging since the summer sun sank into the cerulean sea.

(OWEN changes back to GROPIUS.)

KAI AS ITTEN: Fraulein Stolzl, have you heard of Richard Leutheusser?

(ELLIS AS MAHLER drinks and eyes BREC AS STOLZL.)

BREC AS STOLZL: Oh, he hates us, doesn't

ELLIS AS MAHLER: *(To DUCK AS KANDINSKY)*

he? Some government minister with nothing to do? Do you know what "schmata" means?

KAI AS ITTEN: He seems to have heard about your incident with the begonia.

(DUCK *goes through backpack or bag, retrieves a pitchpipe or an instrument.*)

BREC AS STOLZL: Oh, Master Itten, I am so sorry I fainted! I didn't tell anyone.

KAI AS ITTEN: Maybe another student in the class.

ELLIS AS MAHLER: Johannes, darling, are you making the girls faint again?

KAI AS ITTEN: Does everyone know of this?!

(DUCK *blows the pitchpipe and sings or plays the instrument to accompany* ELLIS AS MAHLER. OWEN AS GROPIUS *observes, finger to temple.*)

ELLIS AS MAHLER/DUCK: (*Singing*)
Itten, Muche, Mazdaznan!
Mazdaznan! Mazdaznan!

(DUCK *puts the pitchpipe or instrument back in the backpack and finds a green envelope, looks puzzled, opens it.*)

OWEN AS GROPIUS: Alma, you're embarrassing yourself! You're drunk!

ELLIS AS MAHLER: I have a beautiful singing voice, everyone says so.

OWEN AS GROPIUS: Go back to Vienna! ELLIS AS MAHLER: I have perfect pitch!

OWEN AS GROPIUS: Go back to Werfel! Go back to your lover!

ELLIS AS MAHLER: He's not my lover! This is my lover!

(ELLIS AS MAHLER *kisses* KAI AS ITTEN, *which is a surprise to everyone.* KAI *pushes* ELLIS *away.*)

KAI: That's not in the script!

OWEN: Indeed it's not!

ELLIS: Look, it was going there—

BREC: Don't say "look".

ELLIS: —And I improvised!   BREC: *(To* KAI*)* That's sexual assault!

DUCK: Excuse, please—

KAI: Mahler's cut! She's a maniac!

BREC: And this depiction is sexist!

ELLIS: She really did those things!

KAI: Not by herself!

BREC: She knows like nothing about design!

KAI: Or painting! She's just a footnote!

OWEN: Agreed! We should focus on the conflict between Gropius and Itten—

KAI: Gropius and the government—

DUCK: Excuse—   ELLIS: I'm the director!

OWEN: And I'm the writer! *(To* KAI*)* You don't even want to do this assignment!

KAI: All right, here we go. I have to goddamn pass, so everybody stop fucking around—!

DUCK: Excuse, please!   ELLIS: If you cut Alma, I'm done. *(Starts to leave)*

BREC: We'll add a Nazi!

ELLIS: If we can empathize with Alma, who is, of course, monstrous—monstrously entertaining—we learn the lessons of history. Alma is history!

OWEN: Indeed she is! I have to do a complete rewrite— from scratch! Throw all of this out! All of it!

ELLIS: We shall see.

DUCK: Excuse the fuck out of me, please!

(*Everyone turns to see* DUCK *holding the green envelope.*)

DUCK: Fuck you very much.

BREC: Nice use of idiom.

DUCK: What mean "pending?"

ELLIS: Pending what?

DUCK: "Expulsion."

(*Silence*)

ELLIS: Well, this is a real nice clambake.

KAI: Expulsion for what?

DUCK: "Ethics violation"?

BREC: TOEFL exam.

DUCK: What this mean?

BREC: Owen.

OWEN: Brec, no.

BREC: It means we have to do this presentation and it has to not suck. In fact, it must be the shit. If we get a good grade, our beloved professor gets Owen a scholarship to stay in school. If not…

(*Irritated, but outed,* OWEN *reveals a green envelope. After a moment everyone else does the same.*)

ELLIS: Lots of famous actors dropped out of school: Halle Berry, Tom Hanks, Leonardo di Caprio, Julia Louis-Dreyfus—

BREC: Artists, too: Jasper Johns, Keith Haring, Yoko Ono—

KAI: Adolf Hitler. (*Pause*) Look, it's not—

BREC, ELLIS & DUCK: Don't say look!

KAI: I say we use the presentation to fuck with the administration, satirize their admission policy—

OWEN: Satirize our expulsion?

ELLIS: Maybe have real costumes—

KAI: Getting kicked out of school isn't life or death—

DUCK: For you. *(Pause)* Excuse please, you go back to parents—

BREC: My mom would die!

OWEN: Not me!

BREC: *(To DUCK)* You're richer than all of us put together!

DUCK: To safe home, to American life, to voting—

DUCK: Bauhaus project make me foolish—how you say? —bold. You—inspire—politic—in me. Design can change world. One person change law. I post criticism—

BREC: Yeah, why'd you do that?

KAI: Government criticism?

ELLIS: Don't blame us—

OWEN: The Bauhaus inspired you?

DUCK: You inspire me, but—

BREC: We did? Holy shit!

DUCK: But my country spy—

OWEN: On you?

DUCK: Add me to list—

ELLIS: On us?

KAI: Nothing's private—

BREC: I saw your posts. They were foolish, risky—

DUCK: Yes! Stupid me! I know you think. I know you right. I go home they kill me maybe.

OWEN: I didn't—

ELLIS: Kill? Oh, my God.

KAI: Of course.

BREC: I'm sorry. I'm a bitch.

Duck: Bauhaus more than just grade. For me.

END OF ACT ONE

ACT TWO

(The nondescript space has been transformed, possibly even representing a different, more formal presentation space. It's now totally Bauhaus, with elements of architecture, furniture, posters, dramatic lighting, perhaps even costumes or tapestries hanging from the walls. It's beautiful in a clean, Bauhaus way, not cluttered, although there may be some evidence of KAI's interest in rhyparography. Bauhaus programs have been placed on every seat in the audience. Music in the Bauhaus style welcomes the theatre patrons back from intermission. A desperate, all-encompassing effort has been made, a gesamtkunstwerk. OWEN AS GROPIUS appears with rolled plans, costumed meticulously in period. GROPIUS—and each of the characters—may have a musical leitmotif, either in period or ironically modern, comically intrusive or subtle and elegant.)

OWEN AS GROPIUS: *(Finger to temple)* Wilkommen. I am Walter Gropius, founding director of the Bauhaus, I think I can say the most influential art and design school…ever.

(A brief slide show of Bauhaus designs is projected behind OWEN AS GROPIUS.)

OWEN AS GROPIUS: It is sans hubris I note that the Bauhaus embodied the optimism of early modernism and today pervades all aspects of the man-made— excuse me—human-made environment, from coffee mugs to skyscrapers. Not limited to a single style, the Bauhaus was rather a commitment to design in service of humanity: beautiful, unadorned, modern. In that very chaotic time, modernism drew the ire of the National Socialists who closed the Bauhaus in 1933 after only fourteen years of existence. But my struggle—*mein kampf*, you might say—began the very first day in 1919.

(DUCK AS LEUTHEUSSER *appears, dressed as a stuffy German bureaucrat with a tight vest, pince-nez glasses and a droopy mustache.*)

DUCK AS LEUTHEUSSER: *(Over-articulating)* Herr Gropius, I understand you've shut down the Grand Ducal School of Arts and Crafts.

OWEN AS GROPIUS: Thank you for welcoming me to Weimar, Herr—?

DUCK AS LEUTHEUSSER: Richard Leutheusser, chairman of the German People's Party of Thuringia.

OWEN AS GROPIUS: My dear Herr Leutheusser, if you represent the Thuringian government that funds our school—

DUCK AS LEUTHEUSSER: I am not presently in the government, sir.

OWEN AS GROPIUS: If you were, you would already know the Bauhaus is designed to elevate the applied arts tradition of the School of Arts and Crafts by blending it with the great German painting and sculpture training of the Weimar Academy of Fine Arts.

DUCK AS LEUTHEUSSER: It is hardly German! Your instructors are Jews and foreigners!

OWEN AS GROPIUS: I've hired no Jews that I'm aware of.

DUCK AS LEUTHEUSSER: Paul Klee!

OWEN AS GROPIUS: He is not a Jew. He is often mistaken for Jewish because he is an intellectual.

DUCK AS LEUTHEUSSER: Wassily Kandinsky is a Bol— Bol—

OWEN AS GROPIUS: *(Whispers)* Bolshevik.

DUCK AS LEUTHEUSSER: Chevrolet!

ELLIS: *(Pops out of nowhere)* Bolshevik! *(Disappears)*

DUCK AS LEUTHEUSSER: Bolshevik!

OWEN AS GROPIUS: Kandinsky is a Russian who fled the Bolshevik Revolution.

DUCK AS LEUTHEUSSER: Kandinsky and Klee founded the Blue Rider, a radical art group that claimed to hear "the apocalyptic horsemen in the air!" You see, I am not a provincial no-nothing you can dismiss as ignorant of the arts. I'm the son of a music teacher, conductor and organist!

OWEN AS GROPIUS: The Blue Rider only lasted until 1914 when the war began, when the apocalyptic horsemen in fact arrived.

DUCK AS LEUTHEUSSER: I once met Neat— Neat—

ELLIS: *(Popping out of nowhere)* Nietzsche!   OWEN AS GROPIUS: *(Whispers)* Nietzsche!

DUCK AS LEUTHEUSSER: I once met Nietzsche!

OWEN AS GROPIUS: Herr Leutheusser, the war has ended, the revolution is over, and we all must work together to heal our country. I share your concern about radical, polarizing politics.

DUCK AS LEUTHEUSSER: You do?

OWEN AS GROPIUS: Absolutely. I assure you, the Bauhaus is resolutely apolitical. We are an art school, nothing more.

DUCK AS LEUTHEUSSER: *(Darkly)* A *modern* art school! *(Disappears)*

OWEN AS GROPIUS: Conflict came not only from without, but also within.

(Lights out on OWEN AS GROPIUS *and up on* BREC AS STOLZL *and* ELLIS AS KIPP, *also perfectly attired for the period.* BREC AS STOLZL *offers* ELLIS AS KIPP *a snack, which they share.)*

BREC AS STOLZL: Maria, I'm anxious for you to meet Johannes Itten.

ELLIS AS KIPP: Who's that?

BREC AS STOLZL: Our best teacher, Swiss, a mystic. We don't have nearly enough girls at the Bauhaus. While you're visiting you can audit Itten's introductory course.

ELLIS AS KIPP: Am I allowed?

BREC AS STOLZL: If Itten says it's all right. He has a powerful presence. Once, in his class, I fainted!

ELLIS AS KIPP: Fainted?

BREC AS STOLZL: He's deeply spiritual and champions individual artistic genius, which means he's in a constant battle with our Director, Walter Gropius.

ELLIS AS KIPP: Why?

BREC AS STOLZL: Oriental Indian mysticism versus technology, art for art's sake versus mass production.

ELLIS AS KIPP: Indian? I thought Herr Itten was Swiss.

BREC AS STOLZL: He has an oriental vibration. Come to class and you'll see!

ELLIS AS KIPP: I look forward to fainting. And vibrating.

(Lights up on OWEN AS GROPIUS *and* ELLIS AS KIPP *and* BREC AS STOLZL *preparing for class.* DUCK *becomes a student,* FRITZ ERTL, *and joins them.* ERTL *has tense, high*

shoulders and always carries a book with a red cover and white spine.)

OWEN AS GROPIUS: Johannes talked me into requiring a six-month introductory course which he soon extended to a year. His notion was to give students a spiritual and artistic enema, purging them of outdated notions and infusing them with his ideals of color and form. He was—I must admit—an extraordinarily charismatic teacher.

(Lights out on OWEN AS GROPIUS and up on KAI AS ITTEN, splendidly austere in a monkish burgundy outfit and glasses with a shaved head. Music [by DUCK] scores the scene. KAI AS ITTEN leads DUCK AS ERTL, ELLIS AS KIPP and BREC AS STOLZL in breathing exercises at first, then adding gestures that they mimic. ITTEN tends to clasp one hand around the other wrist. After a few moments:)

KAI AS ITTEN: Become yellow.

(The students try to mime yellow.)

KAI AS ITTEN: Yellow is a triangle, vehement, agitated.

(They try to embody these qualities. DUCK AS ERTL is pretty literal about it.)

KAI AS ITTEN: Now blue.

(They become blue.)

KAI AS ITTEN: Blue is a circle, symmetrical, full, peaceful.

(Again, DUCK AS ERTL is literal, outlining a circle.)

KAI AS ITTEN: Do not be so literal. Feel the blue, be the circle, don't simply trace it.

(DUCK AS ERTL struggles. ELLIS AS KIPP seems to be enjoying herself.)

KAI AS ITTEN: Now red!

(Dramatic shift in movement. Evident competition between ELLIS AS KIPP *and* BREC AS STOLZL *for* KAI AS ITTEN's *attention. Maybe even jostling.)*

KAI AS ITTEN: Black!

(Shift)

KAI AS ITTEN: Red!

(Shift)

KAI AS ITTEN: Black! Red and black are squares.

(Shift)

KAI AS ITTEN: Squares are death.

(Shift)

KAI AS ITTEN: Death is good.

(Shift)

KAI AS ITTEN: Death is peace.

DUCK AS ERTL: *(Strange, Peter Lorre voice)* I thought blue was peace.

KAI AS ITTEN: You must live the colors, live the shapes before you put them on paper. See how simply Fraulein Kipp does it, and she is only auditing. Merci, Fraulein.

*(*KAI AS ITTEN *gathers two lemons and a green book, placing them on a white plate.* OWEN AS GROPIUS *appears. The students sketch the still life. Another slide show of Bauhaus products as* OWEN AS GROPIUS *speaks.)*

OWEN AS GROPIUS: As Director, I was almost overwhelmed with the responsibility of making sure the students were properly fed and clothed, and in order to maintain adequate funding I continued my architectural practice in Berlin. The Bauhaus grew quickly and by 1921 was internationally known. But we were also under fire from every side, accused by the Constructivists of "making Expressionist jam" and becoming an island of recluses. I began developing an entirely new philosophical basis for our work, which meant I had very little idea what Itten was up to.

DUCK AS ERTL: A still life of book and lemons? This is art instruction?

KAI AS ITTEN: It is not as simple as it seems.

OWEN AS GROPIUS: Itten put in more pedagogic hours than any other instructor, which made him the primary educational influence at the school.

(*The students display their drawings.* KAI AS ITTEN *cuts up one lemon and gives each student a slice. They eat them.*)

OWEN AS GROPIUS: Some felt him almost demonic, with an aura that drew many students to his esoteric religion of Mazdaznan.

KAI AS ITTEN: Taste, savor, absorb. Have your drawings captured the substance of the lemon?

(DUCK AS ERTL *laughs.* BREC AS STOLZL *faints.* ELLIS AS KIPP *comes to her aid. Lights out on everyone but* ELLIS AS KIPP *and* BREC AS STOLZL.)

BREC AS STOLZL: Oh, my, Maria! Did I do it again?

ELLIS AS KIPP: I'm not the fainting type, but Itten's impressive indeed. Will you help me apply to the Bauhaus?

BREC AS STOLZL: Maria, how marvelous! Of course I'll help you. But I'd like your help as well. There's a position opening in textile arts, and I hope you'll support me becoming the first woman to teach at the Bauhaus.

ELLIS AS KIPP: Absolutely, Gunta! How may I do that?

BREC AS STOLZL: You've caught Itten's attention. A word from him to Gropius in my favor…

ELLIS AS KIPP: But I barely know Itten!

BREC AS STOLZL: He knows you. He has seen your soul.

ELLIS AS KIPP: In my triangle dance or my lemon drawing?

(OWEN AS GROPIUS *appears. Lights out on* BREC AS STOLZL.)

OWEN AS GROPIUS: Itten oversaw admissions, which was a mistake on my part as it allowed him to control who could enter the Bauhaus and to make them his own.

(*Lights out on* OWEN AS GROPIUS *and up on* KAI AS ITTEN *sitting Buddha-like, inscrutable.* ELLIS AS KIPP *approaches him.*)

ELLIS AS KIPP: Master Itten.

(KAI AS ITTEN *nods.*)

ELLIS AS KIPP: I'd like your advice about applying for admission to the Bauhaus.

KAI AS ITTEN: Castor oil.

ELLIS AS KIPP: I beg your pardon?

KAI AS ITTEN: For purity.

ELLIS AS KIPP: Oh, a laxative?

KAI AS ITTEN: And fasting.

ELLIS AS KIPP: I see.

KAI AS ITTEN: After a hot bath, rub the body with ashes or charcoal.

ELLIS AS KIPP: Also for purification?

KAI AS ITTEN: Commune with nature.

ELLIS AS KIPP: I enjoy hiking…

KAI AS ITTEN: Give me your hand.

(ELLIS AS KIPP *does.*)

KAI AS ITTEN: Cool. Dry. Clean.

(ELLIS AS KIPP *takes her hand away*)

KAI AS ITTEN: Holy.

(*Lights out on* KAI AS ITTEN *and up on* BREC AS STOLZL.)

BREC AS STOLZL: Mazdaznan!

ELLIS AS KIPP: Before I even apply to the Bauhaus?

BREC AS STOLZL: It's a great compliment!

ELLIS AS KIPP: Why haven't you converted?

BREC AS STOLZL: I may not be strong enough for the discipline.

ELLIS AS KIPP: You are! We could join Mazdaznan together.

BREC AS STOLZL: Maria, I would like to, but I'm thinking of getting married.

ELLIS AS KIPP: To whom?

BREC AS STOLZL: To a man who is not Mazdaznan.

ELLIS AS KIPP: He could join as well!

BREC AS STOLZL: Arieh is from Palestine.

ELLIS AS KIPP: Why would that matter?

(*Lights out on* BREC AS STOLZL *and up on* KAI AS ITTEN.)

KAI AS ITTEN: I am designing the perfect house for the perfect man.

ELLIS AS KIPP: What kind of man?

KAI AS ITTEN: The highest kind. Pure.

ELLIS AS KIPP: Spiritually pure.

KAI AS ITTEN: But also of the body. Mazdaznan seeks health, which is why we must fast and purge. But some defects cannot be purged. They are bred in the bone.

ELLIS AS KIPP: What kind of defects?

KAI AS ITTEN: The purest man is the white man, the Aryan man. This is the highest race, the only race to achieve unity and the balance of the three temperaments, the race that must survive to lead humanity forward. My house is for this superhuman, the House of the White Man.

ELLIS AS KIPP: No other men are allowed in?

KAI AS ITTEN: Only the pure Aryan man.

ELLIS AS KIPP: *(Sitting next to* KAI AS ITTEN*)* What of woman?

KAI AS ITTEN: Woman? *(Smiles his weird smile)* Of course.

ELLIS AS KIPP: *(Taking* KAI AS ITTEN*'s hand)* I'm pansexual.

KAI: *(Taking hand away, breaking character)* What?!

*(*BREC *appears, glaring at* ELLIS. OWEN AS GROPIUS *steps in front of them and gestures to the light booth. Lights out on everyone except* OWEN AS GROPIUS, *who takes a moment before speaking.)*

OWEN AS GROPIUS: Itten wasn't especially interested in design. He saw art as an expression of the unseen. This spiritual approach played well with Feininger, Klee and especially Kandinsky, but not with every student.

*(*DUCK AS ERTL *appears carrying the red and white book.)*

DUCK AS ERTL: Herr Director, I wish to make a formal complaint.

OWEN AS GROPIUS: *(Finger to temple)* Of course, the Bauhaus is constantly improving our teaching. Do you have a suggestion?

DUCK AS ERTL: Have you sat in on Master Itten's introductory course lately?

OWEN AS GROPIUS: I find it's best to simply let our teachers teach.

DUCK AS ERTL: We are not drawing or designing so much as dancing! Breathing! Children's exercises and constant pressure to convert to his nonsense cult!

OWEN AS GROPIUS: I will speak to him. But I must be careful. The Landtag is threatening to reduce our funding and we need to present a united front.

DUCK AS ERTL: Johannes Itten is as great a threat to the Bauhaus as any bureaucrat!

OWEN AS GROPIUS: I have an idea. May I test it on you?

DUCK AS ERTL: Absolutely, Herr Director!

OWEN AS GROPIUS: Now that the Bauhaus is established, I feel we need to be less inward looking, less art for art's sake. Germany is in chaos and we're sketching begonias. We need to serve the people of a modern age.

DUCK AS ERTL: I agree, Herr Director, very much!

OWEN AS GROPIUS: The Bauhaus manifesto describes our aims but it's too long.

DUCK AS ERTL: It's a manifesto.

OWEN AS GROPIUS: We need something shorter, that sums up the Bauhaus in a few words, is forward-looking, outward facing. German industry is starting to pick up. We need to embrace technology, design for the masses, infuse human intuition into machine-made products. Generate more income from the workshops with a new economic model.

DUCK AS ERTL: Yes, yes!

OWEN AS GROPIUS: Only an artist can breathe life into an inert, machine-made object, give it a soul.

DUCK AS ERTL: What is this new philosophy?

OWEN AS GROPIUS: Art and technology: a new unity.

DUCK AS ERTL: It is certainly modern.

OWEN AS GROPIUS: But not spiritual in the traditional sense.

DUCK AS ERTL: Itten would hate it very much.

OWEN AS GROPIUS: Yes, I think so.

(Sound of singing as lights go out on OWEN AS GROPIUS *and* DUCK AS ERTL *and come up on* BREC AS STOLZL *and* ELLIS AS KIPP *strolling through the streets of Weimar. They are dressed in Mazdaznan outfits like the one* ITTEN *wears.)*

BREC AS STOLZL/ELLIS AS KIPP: *(Singing)*
Itten, Muche, Mazdaznan!
Mazdaznan! Mazdaznan!

*(*KAI AS ITTEN *appears.)*

BREC AS STOLZL: Master Itten!

KAI AS ITTEN: How wonderful to hear such jubilation. But in the streets of Weimar we must not offend the nonbelievers. Be respectful, be silent, be pleasant.

ELLIS AS KIPP: Yes, Master Itten.

KAI AS ITTEN: And above all, smile! It shows the outer world our inner peace.

*(*KAI AS ITTEN *smiles his weird, fixed smile.* ELLIS AS KIPP *and* BREC AS STOLZL *follow suit.* DUCK AS LEUTHEUSSER *appears, and they turn their smiles toward him.)*

DUCK AS LEUTHEUSSER: *Gott in Himmel! (Flees)*

KAI AS ITTEN: Weimar is stuck in the spiritual past. It may not be the best place for us.

BREC AS STOLZL: The Bauhaus is here in Weimar.

KAI AS ITTEN: But Mazdaznan is in America.

ELLIS AS KIPP: America?

KAI AS ITTEN: The headquarters of Mazdaznan moved to Los Angeles a few years ago.

BREC AS STOLZL: Hollywood? The opposite of spiritual!

KAI AS ITTEN: Perhaps the spiritual realm has conspired to bring us together today outside the walls of the Bauhaus. May I ask you something in confidence?

BREC AS STOLZL: Of course, Master Itten!

ELLIS AS KIPP: Certainly!

(They edge closer together, ELLIS AS KIPP *and* BREC AS STOLZL *competing to be closer to* KAI AS ITTEN.*)*

KAI AS ITTEN: I am only thinking of emigrating as a last resort. I'd much prefer staying at the Bauhaus to save it.

BREC AS STOLZL: Is the Bauhaus in danger?

KAI AS ITTEN: We shall save the Bauhaus from itself—through Mazdaznan which must become the official doctrine of the Bauhaus!

ELLIS AS KIPP: We've converted!

KAI AS ITTEN: But devotion is not enough. Now we must take action. May I speak frankly?

(They lean in)

KAI AS ITTEN: We must expose that pawn of commercialism, Walter Gropius!

ELLIS AS KIPP: Expose Gropius?

BREC AS STOLZL: The Director?

KAI AS ITTEN: Yes. He forces students to work on his architectural commissions and spends too much time in Berlin.

BREC AS STOLZL: Expose him…how?

KAI AS ITTEN: Every student has come through the introductory course, their taste and skill formed by my methods.

BREC AS STOLZL/ELLIS AS KIPP: We have!

KAI AS ITTEN: I've turned the whole school into a fluid entity, something I can manipulate into a new direction.

BREC AS STOLZL: To what end, Master Itten?

KAI AS ITTEN: Can't you feel it? The entire nation is in thrall to the German mystics. The time has come!

ELLIS AS KIPP: Time for what?

KAI AS ITTEN: Time for me to become the Director of the Bauhaus!

(*Both* BREC AS STOLZL *and* ELLIS AS KIPP *faint. Lights out on them and up on* OWEN AS GROPIUS *and* DUCK AS LEUTHEUSSER.)

OWEN AS GROPIUS: (*Finger to temple*) Fire Itten?

DUCK AS LEUTHEUSSER: Otherwise, as a tax-paying citizen, I will request an audit of Bauhaus finances.

OWEN AS GROPIUS: Finances? There are none!

DUCK AS LEUTHEUSSER: And an exhibition of Bauhaus products that demonstrate your financial viability.

OWEN AS GROPIUS: An exhibition? To justify our existence?

DUCK AS LEUTHEUSSER: You are funded by the State of Thuringia, wasting German marks on debauched costume parties, nude bathing in the river, and Semitic rituals.

OWEN AS GROPIUS: Semitic rituals?

DUCK AS LEUTHEUSSER: Itten stalks about town robed like a mad rabbi! Smiling an idiotic, vacant smile.

OWEN AS GROPIUS: Itten isn't Jewish, he's Mazdaznan.

DUCK AS LEUTHEUSSER: Which has unChristian oriental roots!

OWEN AS GROPIUS: Christianity has oriental roots. And Itten himself is an anti-Semite!

DUCK AS LEUTHEUSSER: How do you know?

(Lights up on BREC AS STOLZL, *no longer in Mazdaznan attire.)*

BREC AS STOLZL: *(Quiet and sad)* I am Judas.

OWEN AS GROPIUS: Whom do you betray?

BREC AS STOLZL: Master Itten. He's forbidden me to become Mazdaznan because I'm marrying Arieh Sharon.

OWEN AS GROPIUS: The Palestinian architect?

BREC AS STOLZL: I will lose German citizenship.

OWEN AS GROPIUS: What business is this of mine?

BREC AS STOLZL: Itten plans to take over the Bauhaus.

OWEN AS GROPIUS: This is not news, Gunta. That's been his goal since my ex-wife persuaded me to hire him.

*(*ELLIS AS MAHLER *suddenly swoops in, and steps into the light for a moment. This is the most fully realized costume yet, very detailed.)*

ELLIS AS MAHLER: So many fine and famous artists at the Weimar Bauhaus: Paul Klee, Wassily Kandinsky, Oskar Schlemmer, Marcel Breuer, Lyonel Feininger, Georg Muche, Herbert Bayer and Gerhardt Marcks. But really the Bauhaus was the creation of just two men: Walter Gropius and Johannes Itten, both there thanks to me, Alma Mahler Gropius Werfel. But pay me no mind. I am just a footnote! *(Disappears)*

(This was not supposed to happen. DUCK, OWEN *and* BREC *are shocked for a moment and almost break character, but*

recover and resume their roles as LEUTHEUSSER, GROPIUS *and* STOLZL.*)*

OWEN AS GROPIUS: *(Fingers to temples)* Do not worry, Gunta. I have a plan for Itten.

*(*BREC AS STOLZL *sobs and the light on her goes out.)*

DUCK AS LEUTHEUSSER: You will fire him?

OWEN AS GROPIUS: If this were fascist Italy and I Mussolini, I'd resort to a brutal firing. But this is Germany.

(Lights out on DUCK AS LEUTHEUSSER *and up on* KAI AS ITTEN.*)*

KAI AS ITTEN: You're making Gunta Stolzl a Master?

OWEN AS GROPIUS: To head up the weaving studio.

KAI AS ITTEN: With all due respect…a woman?

OWEN AS GROPIUS: It's only weaving.

KAI AS ITTEN: She's marrying a Jew.

OWEN AS GROPIUS: What business is that of mine? Or yours?

KAI AS ITTEN: It will be used against the Bauhaus.

OWEN AS GROPIUS: As you've used it against her?

KAI AS ITTEN: *(Turns to the audience)* Gropius appears to be taking a pious stance, but he was also a product of his time and as anti-Semitic as anyone else in the Weimar period.

(Like the MAHLER *interruption, this was also not supposed to happen.)*

OWEN AS GROPIUS: Johannes, what are you—?

KAI AS ITTEN: When his wife Alma Mahler Gropius cheated on him with the writer Franz Werfel—

OWEN AS GROPIUS: We are no longer married!

KAI AS ITTEN: OWEN AS GROPIUS:
Gropius told Alma he   What business is it of
was repulsed to think of   mine?
the circumcised penises
of Gustav Mahler and
Franz Werfel entering his
wife.

OWEN: *(Sotto voce)* Kai, stick to the script!

KAI: Just telling the truth, Owen!

*(*KAI *smiles the scary* ITTEN *smile and returns to character.* OWEN, *rattled, takes a bit longer to return to character as* GROPIUS.)*

OWEN AS GROPIUS: Johannes, I'm reducing your course load. You've firmly established the introductory class, so you can move on to higher level students—

KAI AS ITTEN: The introductory course is mine! I invented it!

OWEN AS GROPIUS: Now it's time for others to take forward your outstanding work on color theory—

KAI AS ITTEN: I invented the color wheel!

OWEN AS GROPIUS: We are being audited because of you, and forced to throw together an exhibition that proves our worth. Mazdaznan has gone too far. Even your disciple Georg Muche is disturbed by your racist writings.

KAI AS ITTEN: Isn't it interesting that racists are always the first to accuse someone else of racism?

OWEN AS GROPIUS: Order your steps, Johannes.

KAI AS ITTEN: All right, here we go.

(Lighting change puts KAI AS ITTEN *in the dark and illuminates* DUCK AS KANDINSKY, *wearing the cardigan with ramrod posture.)*

OWEN AS GROPIUS: Itten pulled out the big guns: Wassily Kandinsky and Paul Klee.

(OWEN *becomes* KLEE, *holding a pipe.*)

DUCK AS KANDINSKY: Gropius, art is to suck hind tit? Teapots, table lamps and lounge chairs now more important than painting? Individuality is the future! The collective is the past!

OWEN AS KLEE: Art and technology: a new unity. A new outrage!

(Lights out on DUCK AS KANDINSKY *and* OWEN AS KLEE *and up on* KAI AS ITTEN *teaching* ELLIS AS KIPP *and* BREC AS STOLZL, *who both have sketchpads.)*

KAI AS ITTEN: In our continued analysis of old masters—

DUCK AS ERTL: *(Arriving late and irritated)* I hate art history—history is boring!

KAI AS ITTEN: Everything that ever happened is boring? Because that is history. But in any case, I remind you that we are not studying art history. We are developing sensitivity to contrasts through the experience of intense empathy.

(KAI AS ITTEN *unveils a reproduction of a painting [not necessarily seen by the audience] and the students begin scribbling.)*

KAI AS ITTEN: *(Working himself into frenzy)* Can you truly capture on paper the light, the dark, the relationships, the weight, the rhythm of the Isenheim Altarpiece by Matthias Grünewald? The writhing agony of the Christ, the unspeakable sorrow of the weeping Magdalen— *(Roars)* If you had the tiniest inkling of an artistic temperament, you couldn't possibly sit there drawing—drawing!—before this sublime embodiment of grief, the devastation of the world—you would be melting into tears yourselves, you heartless—

(KAI AS ITTEN *utters a kind of screaming groan, runs out and slams the door loudly behind him.* ELLIS AS KIPP, BREC AS STOLZL *and* DUCK AS ERTL *promptly faint and fall to the floor.* DUCK *is the first to recover, stands and becomes* LEUTHEUSSER *[adding pince-nez glasses and mustache].* DUCK AS LEUTHEUSSER *helps* BREC AS STOLZL *to her feet.)*

DUCK AS LEUTHEUSSER: Fraulein Stolzl, you fainted in class?

BREC AS STOLZL: Who are you?

(ELLIS AS KIPP *pulls herself to her feet unassisted and gathers her sketches.)*

DUCK AS LEUTHEUSSER: Richard Leutheusser, a candidate for the presidency of the Thuringia Landtag. *(Gives her a campaign leaflet)* I'm running on a traditional German platform.

(While BREC AS STOLZL *reads the leaflet,* DUCK *becomes* ERTL *and turns imperiously toward* ELLIS AS KIPP.*)*

ELLIS AS KIPP: I'm applying for admission. May I show my work to Master Itten?

DUCK AS ERTL: The Master has entrusted me with your application.

ELLIS AS KIPP: I thought you hated him!

DUCK AS ERTL: Like Paul on the road to Damascus, I fell blind but have seen the light.

*(*ELLIS AS KIPP *hands her sketches to* DUCK AS ERTL, *who clutches them to his chest but does not look at them.)*

BREC AS STOLZL: But how did you hear I fainted?

DUCK AS LEUTHEUSSER: *(Turning to* BREC AS STOLZL*)* You must report Itten to the Director.

BREC AS STOLZL: I've said too much already. How does everyone know about my fainting?!

DUCK AS LEUTHEUSSER: I'm very likely to be elected, which means Director Gropius would appreciate your report.

BREC AS STOLZL: I don't understand.

DUCK AS LEUTHEUSSER: As president of the Landtag, I will oversee the Bauhaus allocation. And I regard your Master Itten as a foreign threat to Thuringia.

BREC AS STOLZL: Herr Leutheusser, you're putting me in a terrible position!

ELLIS AS KIPP: Herr Ertl? Are you going to review my work?

(DUCK becomes ERTL and turns toward ELLIS AS KIPP but doesn't look at her or her sketches.)

BREC AS STOLZL: Herr Leutheusser?

ELLIS AS KIPP: Herr Ertl? Are you all right? Fritz?

(Lights out on BREC AS STOLZL.)

DUCK AS ERTL: You…are…accepted!

(Both ELLIS AS KIPP and DUCK AS ERTL faint. Lights out on them and up on OWEN AS GROPIUS and KAI AS ITTEN.)

OWEN AS GROPIUS: Did you vote?

KAI AS ITTEN: I am not registered to vote in Germany.

OWEN AS GROPIUS: *(Finger to temple)* Ach, I forgot you're still Swiss.

KAI AS ITTEN: But I never vote in Switzerland either. What good does it do?

OWEN AS GROPIUS: Perhaps your vote would have prevented Richard Leutheusser from becoming president of the Thuringia Landtag.

KAI AS ITTEN: What do German provincial politics have to do with me?

OWEN AS GROPIUS: With students continually fainting in your class it was already hard to defend you to the government. Now Leutheusser *is* the government, and he's heard about the Grünewald Altarpiece.

DUCK AS LEUTHEUSSER: *(Appearing)* That Swiss madman screamed at the students, ran out and slammed the door behind him. The whole class was traumatized! German taxes paid for this nonsense!

(DUCK AS LEUTHEUSSER *disappears.*)

KAI AS ITTEN: They sat before one of the world's greatest artworks unmoved!

OWEN AS GROPIUS: Your behavior to the students is abusive.

KAI AS ITTEN: They're the students! I'm the Master!

OWEN AS GROPIUS: A Master. One of several. I am the only Director.

KAI AS ITTEN: Then why—with all due respect—are you so often in Berlin?

OWEN AS GROPIUS: My architectural practice supports the Bauhaus.

KAI AS ITTEN: Bauhaus students labor on your commissions.

OWEN AS GROPIUS: They are paid!

KAI AS ITTEN: I see. Will that be all, Herr Director?

OWEN AS GROPIUS: No. I've decided I must approve all student admissions. In just a few years of existence, the Bauhaus has developed an international reputation—

KAI AS ITTEN: With my instructional expertise—!

OWEN AS GROPIUS: A reputation I must uphold with the highest admission standards. I understand a Fraulein— *(Consults paper)* Maria Kipp has just been admitted. What are her qualifications?

KAI AS ITTEN: She is an intuitive artist—

OWEN AS GROPIUS: Her background, previous schooling—?

KAI AS ITTEN: Sensitive to shapes and colors—

OWEN AS GROPIUS: You don't know because you authorized your Mazdaznan acolyte Fritz Ertl to review her application in your stead.

KAI AS ITTEN: He is also quite sensitive.

OWEN AS GROPIUS: Susceptible to fainting, I understand. Like many Mazdaznan students. Like Maria Kipp.

KAI AS ITTEN: This is pure pettiness!

(ELLIS AS MAHLER *bursts in, a surprise to both* KAI *and* OWEN.)

ELLIS AS MAHLER: Gropius is prone to pettiness!

OWEN AS GROPIUS: (*Trying to stay in character*) Alma, what are you doing here? We've been divorced a year!

ELLIS AS MAHLER: And he's always envied your attractiveness to women!

(ELLIS AS MAHLER *tries to kiss* KAI AS ITTEN, *who fights her off, but maybe she gets her kiss first.*)

OWEN AS GROPIUS:	KAI:
Alma, you're mad!	Ellis, you freak, get off me!

(OWEN AS GROPIUS *gestures frantically to the light booth, but the lights stay on.*)

ELLIS AS MAHLER: Your petty squabbles mean nothing now. This exhibition is a trap. The Bauhaus is doomed!

(ELLIS AS MAHLER *disappears.* OWEN *and* KAI *take a moment to recover and return to character.*)

KAI AS ITTEN: Your leadership is weak. You kowtow to the Landtag—

OWEN AS GROPIUS: The Landtag is our patron! Our primary funder!

KAI AS ITTEN: You're unprincipled and lack vision. You're not even an artist!

OWEN AS GROPIUS: I'm an architect!

KAI AS ITTEN: The Bauhaus is in chaos! I'm tempted to tender my resignation—!

OWEN AS GROPIUS: Accepted!

KAI AS ITTEN: What?

OWEN AS GROPIUS: I accept your resignation. *(Sincerely, fingers to temples)* With all due respect.

*(*KAI AS ITTEN *blinks, stunned. Lights out on him and* OWEN AS GROPIUS, *and up on* BREC AS STOLZL *and* ELLIS AS KIPP.)*

BREC AS STOLZL: Gropius rejected you?

ELLIS AS KIPP: After I'd been admitted to the Bauhaus!

BREC AS STOLZL: He's just made me a Master. I'll appeal to him.

ELLIS AS KIPP: It's not about me or my talent as a weaver, is it?

BREC AS STOLZL: You're very talented, Maria!

ELLIS AS KIPP: I was a pawn.

BREC AS STOLZL: Me, too. I'm so ashamed.

ELLIS AS KIPP: Gropius is desperate to defend the Bauhaus from criticism. Even Itten was a pawn of sorts.

BREC AS STOLZL: Perhaps if you hadn't become Mazdaznan…

ELLIS AS KIPP: Mazdaznan is more than just a way to get in the school. It guides everything I am now. Don't appeal to Gropius. I, at least, do not wish to be desperate and pathetic. Some day I'll show him I don't need his little Bauhaus.

BREC AS STOLZL: What will you do?

ELLIS AS KIPP: Go back to Erich in Munich, I imagine.

BREC AS STOLZL: Maybe you could teach at the *Kunstgewerbeschule* or start your own textile studio.

ELLIS AS KIPP: Or move to Los Angeles where Mazdaznan is headquartered.

BREC AS STOLZL: Los Angeles!?

(*Lights out on them and up on* DUCK AS LEUTHEUSSER *and* OWEN AS GROPIUS.)

DUCK AS LEUTHEUSSER: Our audit has determined that the Bauhaus is financially unstable. Delinquent payments—

OWEN AS GROPIUS: The workshops have been—

DUCK AS LEUTHEUSSER: Ethics violations—

OWEN AS GROPIUS: —Forced to produce everything from nothing, purchase raw materials in uneconomically small quantities. We can't compete with industry because we can't afford machines—

DUCK AS LEUTHEUSSER: Your exhibition was too abstract to be practical.

OWEN AS GROPIUS: We've received industrial orders based on the exhibition, but inflation has wiped out any chance of profits—

DUCK AS LEUTHEUSSER: You've had six years to prove yourselves.

OWEN AS GROPIUS: This open hostility—artistic intolerance and lack of understanding—has made it doubly difficult to develop a solid business enterprise—

Duck as Leutheusser: This month instructors salaries will be reduced by half—

Owen as Gropius:
They cannot survive on—

Duck as Leutheusser:
Pending termination—

Duck as Leutheusser: In six months all employment will be terminated.

Owen as Gropius: All?

Duck as Leutheusser: Yours included, Herr Director. This is the end of the Bauhaus.

(Lights out on Duck as Leutheusser.*)*

Owen as Gropius: *(Fingers to temples)* And so it was... for a few months. But such a school could not die. The fame of the Bauhaus internationally and throughout Germany made us attractive to less conservative governments, including the city of Dessau. In 1925 the mayor, Fritz Hesse, became our champion, and not only agreed to fund the Bauhaus but also to support a new facility in Dessau that I designed as well as beautiful new homes for all the Masters.

*(*Ellis *appears dressed as* Adolf Hitler, *slowly and ominously edging into the light, complete with swastika armband.)*

Owen as Gropius: Rising like a phoenix, like Germany itself recovering from the war— *(He starts to notice* Ellis.*)* —The Bauhaus began a glorious period of reinvention and artistic influence—

*(*Ellis *steps fully into the light.* Owen *is forced to break character by the spectacle of* Hitler *invading the stage.)*

Owen: Bloody hell!

Ellis as Hitler: Instruction in world history at the so-called high schools is in a very sorry condition. Few teachers understand that the study of history can never be to learn historical dates and events by heart and recite them by rote. To "earn" history means to identify the forces which cause those effects we subsequently perceive as historical events.

(BREC *appears, eating something, observing* ELLIS, *furious.*)

ELLIS AS HITLER: Germany must never forget the causes of its humiliation and betrayal at Versailles. The man who has no sense of history, is like a man who has no ears or eyes. Never forget!

(BREC *tackles* ELLIS. OWEN *gestures to the light booth and there is an instant blackout.*)

OWEN: *(In the dark)* Ellis, Brec, you've both gone quite mad!

(*Sounds of confusion in the darkness. Eventually the lights come up on* DUCK, BREC *and* KAI *waiting nervously.* BREC *and* KAI *are holding hands.* ELLIS *sits a bit apart, still dressed as Hitler, bleeding from a small head wound.*)

BREC: *(After an uncomfortable pause)* Where did you even get—?

ELLIS: The theatre department did *The Producers* a few years ago—

KAI: What the fuck were you thinking?

DUCK: We get expel!

BREC: All that work, planning, and then you— improvise—!

DUCK: I go back my country, get torture!

DUCK: Kill!   KAI: So selfish—!

BREC: This was a group project! Everyone had a role, but yours wasn't big enough, so you pop back in as Alma Mahler—

KAI: And fucking Adolf   BREC: Playing dress-up!
Hitler!

ELLIS: The climax was weak! Narration of a happy ending—!

DUCK: Three people walk out—!

KAI: My room-mate was very offended—

BREC: There should have been a trigger warning—

BREC: You can't have Hitler say never forget!

ELLIS: He said it! All that was a quote!

BREC: Are you Jewish?

ELLIS: No…

BREC: Exactly!

ELLIS: What?

(OWEN *appears. Everyone stares apprehensively.*)

OWEN: We are all still on probation. But we can stay another term.

KAI: Just one?

BREC: Probation because of Hitler? Or crazy ho Alma kissing on everybody?

OWEN: The administration was impressed with the presentation overall but "concerned" by Der Fuhrer. Apparently there's been some negative national attention.

ELLIS: Already?

KAI: See?

BREC: (*To* DUCK *then* ELLIS) Did you Tweet? Did you?

OWEN: And we will be required to make a formal apology to the school.

ELLIS: God!

OWEN: Apparently a special appeal was made—

DUCK: By beloved professor?

OWEN: Yes.

KAI: He saved our asses.

DUCK: Can you help me apply grad school?

(KAI *just laughs, astonished.*)

BREC: Still, it's creepy.

ELLIS: We get to stay, y'all! Chill out!

DUCK: No kill!

OWEN: However.

BREC: What?

KAI: Fuck me.

DUCK: Oh, no.

OWEN: We have to do another project next term.

KAI: *Jugendstijl tableaux vivantes*?

BREC: German Expressionist, like, opera?

KAI: Art Deco puppets?

ELLIS: What?

OWEN: Bauhaus part two: Dessau.

KAI: Holy fucking crap!

BREC: And you got your scholarship, didn't you?

OWEN: Also just one term.

ELLIS: The Bauhaus was in Dessau what years?

BREC: Why does that matter?   OWEN: From 1925 through 1932.

ELLIS: Nineteen thirty-two? The year before Hitler became Chancellor—?

OWEN: Yes, this next one can have Nazis.

OWEN/KAI/BREC/DUCK: But no Alma Mahler!

ELLIS: We shall see.

END OF PLAY

www.ingramcontent.com/pod-product-compliance
Lightning Source LLC
Chambersburg PA
CBHW061617130726
47996CB00003B/1018